LE

Things Done with Words:
Speech Acts in
Hispanic Drama

Things Done With Words:
Speech Acts in Hispanic Drama

Proceedings of the 1984 Stony Brook Seminar

Edited by

ELIAS L. RIVERS

Juan de la Cuesta
Newark, Delaware

MANUFACTURED IN THE UNITED STATES OF AMERICA

The pH of the paper this book is printed on is 7.00 or slightly
higher.

ISBN: 0-936388-26-9

Contents

PREFACE

DURING THE SUMMER OF 1984, on the campus of the State University of New York at Stony Brook, Long Island, I had the opportunity to direct an unusually productive seminar funded by the National Endowment for the Humanities. A dozen college professors from different parts of the country read with me a selection of plays, both classical and modern, written in Spanish. With the help of ideas about language as action that have developed out of J. L. Austin's *How to Do Things with Words*, we discussed at length and in detail how verbal transactions constitute not only the substance of social life, but also the structure of dramatic texts and of their theatrical representations. We found, for instance, that the Spanish honor code, foregrounded in many classical plays, provides excellent examples of rule-constituted language games and ritualistic speech acts. The underlying threat of physical violence is normally controlled by a system of verbal authority; but any crisis within this system makes dramatic characters explicitly conscious of how words work, and fail to work.

Having developed in an exploratory way a tentative consensus concerning dramatic speech acts, members of the seminar analyzed a series of different plays. This collection of essays is the result of our collective and individual labors. It is, I believe, a highly coherent collection; in fact, certain basic ideas are frequently returned to from different points of view. I have invited one of our guest speakers, Professor Inés Azar, to write an introduction, providing a general perspective upon the intrinsic speech-act structure of dramatic works. A member of the seminar, Professor Albert Prince, has written a general theoretical conclusion. Knowing from experience how fruitful the exchange of ideas was within our small group, I am confident that the publication of this volume will provoke productive discussion within the larger community of those who teach drama and try to analyze dramatic structure in a systematic way.

I am grateful to the National Endowment for the Humanities for its financial support. I am also grateful to all of our guest speakers— Professor Pedro Lastra, Professor Enrique Giordano, Professor Jan Kott—and to all the members of our seminar for their unusually productive collaboration in critical theory and practice. Special thanks are due to Professor Inés Azar and Professor Albert Prince for their stimulating oral discussions and for their written contributions to this volume.

Finally, I thank Dean Don Ihde of the State University of New York at Stony Brook, for authorizing a subvention making possible the publication of this volume.

Spring of 1985   ELIAS RIVERS
Stony Brook

Things Done with Words:
Speech Acts in
Hispanic Drama

Self, Responsibility, Discourse:
an Introduction to
Speech Act Theory

INÉS AZAR

Accuracy and morality alike are on the side of the plain
saying that *our word is our bond.*

JOHN L. AUSTIN
How to Do Things With Words

So you are saying that human agreement decides what is true
and what is false?—It is what human beings *say* that is true
and false, and they agree in the *language* they use. That is not
agreement in opinions but in form of life.

LUDWIG WITTGENSTEIN
Philosophical Investigations

May we compete with one another,
Cooperating in this competition
Until our naming
Gives voice correctly.
And how things are
And how we say things are
Are one.

KENNETH BURKE
"Dialectician's Hymn"

ONG BEFORE I knew about Speech Act Theory,
the dialogue of *La Celestina* had struck me as
remarkable in its insistence on examining itself
as dialogue. Such self-referentiality can only be
achieved by making characters, even secondary
ones, unusually aware of the uses of language,
its powers and its traps. Yet, the dialogue of *La
Celestina* is made out of a fundamental paradox:
for all their lucidity, its characters are no less vulnerable to the
linguistic manipulations they are able to uncover and willing to
denounce. Pármeno, for instance, repeatedly warns Calisto against

believing any of Celestina's promises, though he himself takes her at her word when she says what he wants to hear. Sempronio denounces in numerous asides the inanity of his master's courtly language but becomes hopelessly courtly and inane in front of the prostitute he is in love with. With their unusual critical abilities and their linguistic theorizing, the characters of La Celestina do not enhance communication but make its failure all the more radical. They are all haunted and in the end undone by language. Not even Celestina, who embodies the powers of the word, escapes this fate.

As in La Celestina, in Shakespeare's Coriolanus personal fate depends almost exclusively on linguistic behavior. This is why Stanley Fish finds Speech Act Theory particularly suited to study Shakespeare's play:[1]

> Thus simply by paying attention to the hero's illocutionary behavior and then referring to the full dress accounts of the acts he performs, it is possible to produce a speech act "reading" of the play.... To the extent that this reading is satisfying, it is because Coriolanus is a Speech Act play. That is to say, it is about what the theory is "about," the conditions for the successful performance of certain conventional acts and the commitments one enters into or avoids by performing or refusing to perform those acts (1001-1002).

Of course, the same argument could be made in the case of La Celestina. Yet, I will claim for the theory exactly what Fish denies it: that it does provide critics with useful strategies to analyze literary texts, be they or not about "what the theory is about."

The theory of speech acts was first formulated by John Austin. In How To Do Things With Words, Austin sets out to distinguish performative from constative utterances.[2] Constatives report or describe states of affairs that exist "in the world," prior to discourse and independent of it: "Rojas wrote La Celestina"; "A promise is a speech act." Constatives are referential and therefore have truth-values: if the words fit the world, the given statement is true; if they do not, the statement is false.

Performatives, on the other hand, are not referential in the way constatives are. When the president of the United States says, for instance, "I hereby declare a state of emergency," he is not reporting or describing a condition that existed prior to his declaration, although some specific condition must exist for his declaration to be at all possible and appropriate. In declaring a state of emergency, the president is bringing such a state into existence.

---

[1] Stanley Fish, "How to Do Things With Austin and Searle: Speech Act Theory and Literary Criticism," MLN 91 (1976), 983-1025.

[2] John L. Austin, How to Do Things With Words (Cambridge, Mass.: Harvard University Press, 1975), pp. 1-24.

Since performatives create the state of affairs to which they refer, they are neither true nor false, but they can be well performed or defective in a number of ways:

There must exist an accepted conventional procedure having a certain conventional effect, that procedure to include the uttering of certain words by certain persons in certain circumstances, and further, the particular persons and circumstances in a given case must be appropriate for the invocation of the particular procedure invoked (Austin, 14-15).

If, for example, when the president-elect has to take the oath of office he says "I proclaim" instead of the prescribed "I swear" or "I affirm," he would be saying and doing something, but he would not be taking the oath of office.

At the start Austin opposes performatives to constatives as doing something versus saying something; yet he ends by finding such opposition to be unworkable. In the process of building and, in the end, undoing his original distinction, Austin formulates his theory of illocutionary acts: all discourse is action; every utterance is an act; though different in kind, performatives and constatives are both speech acts (Austin, 133-147).

In *Speech Acts* John Searle develops Austin's last formulation.[3] According to Searle, the theory is based on a single hypothesis: to speak a language is to engage in a highly complex form of intentional behavior not simply regulated but created by rules. Specifically, speaking a language is performing speech acts—acts such as making statements, asking questions, giving commands, and so on. The unit of linguistic communication is not the word or the sentence but the speech act.[4]

---

[3] John R. Searle, *Speech Acts* (Cambridge: Cambridge University Press, 1969), pp. 1-21. All references are to this book, except for the one in note 5 below.

[4] Dell Hymes, *Foundations in Sociolinguistics* (Philadelphia: University of Pennsylvania Press, 1974), pp. 52-53: "The speech act... represents a level distinct from the sentence, and not identifiable with any single portion of other levels of grammar, nor with segments of any particular size defined in terms of other levels of grammar. That an utterance has the status of a command may depend upon a conventional formula ("I hereby order you to leave this building"), intonation ("Go!" vs. "Go?"), position in a conversational exchange ("Hello" as initiating greeting or as response, as when answering the telephone), and the social relationship obtaining between the parties (as when an utterance that is in form a polite question is in effect a command, when made by a superior to a subordinate). In general the relation between sentence forms and speech acts is of the kind just mentioned: a sentence interrogative in form may be now a request, now a command, now a statement; a request may be manifested by a sentence that is now interrogative, now declarative, now imperative in form: and one and the same sentence may be taken as a promise or as a threat, depending on the norm of interpretation applied to it." For an

Speech acts are successfully performed and understood only if certain conditions obtain. Such conditions include the *psychological state* expressed in the utterance (*sincerity* condition), the *interest, status* and *relative position of speaker and listener* (different types of *preparatory* conditions) and the *point* of the speech act (*essential* condition). Commands and requests, for instance, have identical essential and sincerity conditions; they also have the same preparatory conditions except for the one that describes the relative position of speaker and listener: for a command, the speaker must be in a position of authority; for a request, the listener must have some measure of authority or he and the speaker must be equals.

Different kinds of speech acts may have similar preparatory or sincerity conditions. The essential condition is the one that distinguishes and defines the kinds. Thus, commands and requests are *directive* speech acts; promises and threats are *commissives*. The essential condition of a directive is that it counts as an attempt by the speaker to get the listener to do something. The essential condition of a commissive is that it counts as the undertaking of an obligation by the speaker to make some of his future acts match his present words (Searle, 64-71).[5]

Stanley Fish has pointed out that the expression "counts as" reveals the theory's position on intention: in the view of Speech Act Theory, intention "is a matter of what one takes responsibility for by performing certain conventional (speech) acts" (Fish, 986). The question of what is going on inside is bypassed:

Wherever there is a psychological state specified in the sincerity condition, the performance of the act counts as an expression of that psycological state. This law holds whether the act is sincere or insincere, that is whether the speaker actually has the specified state or not (Searle, 65).

The theory's view on intention can not—and should not—be isolated from its view on convention: "The [illocutionary] act is constituted not by intention or by fact, essentially but by *convention* (which is, of course, a fact)" (Austin, 128)

In his analysis of Shakespeare's *Coriolanus* Fish argues convincingly that the problem of the protagonist is precisely his position on intention: for Coriolanus nothing can "count as" anything unless it is validated by what is going on inside. The entire course of the tragedy is the unfolding of Coriolanus' linguistic behavior and of its necessary consequences. Coriolanus is proud of his patrician origins, and even

---

instance of the same sentence taken first as a promise and immediately after as a threat, see below pp. xiii-xv.

[5] Cf. John R. Searle, "A Taxonomy of Illucutionary Acts," in *Expression and Meaning* (Cambridge: Cambridge University Press, 1979), chapter I, pp. 1-29.

prouder of his exceptional performance as a soldier. As intense as his pride is his contempt for the common people, those who can claim neither ancestry nor bravery as their merit. Both his pride and his contempt are dramatically exposed in the opening scenes and developed through the play up to their climax in the scene of his banishment.

From the beginning, Coriolanus is depicted as deserving public recognition (a consulship) for his military prowess (the defeat of Aufidius and the Volsces at Corioli). Yet, also from the beginning, Coriolanus appears to be unable or unwilling to make requests or accept praise, which is, however, what he must do if he is to become a consul. In act II, the tribune Sicinius accurately predicts:[6]

May they perceive's intent! He will require them
As if he did contemn what he requested
Should be in them to give. (ii, 181)

One of the preparatory conditions of requesting is that the speaker believes his listener is able to act as requested. Without such belief only a mock request could be issued. And this is exactly what happens: Coriolanus invalidates his request by making it in such a way that he denies the right and ability of the people to certify his merit. For Coriolanus, true merit—his merit—is self-validating: he can accept no authority other than himself.

Fish shows that Coriolanus is constantly asserting his independence from the shared system of conventional speech acts. Coriolanus's illocutionary behavior is monolithic; he not only refuses to accept the public procedure by which the state determines value but, shortly before his banishment, he declares:

I would not buy
Their mercy at the price of one fair word,
Nor check my courage for what they can give,
To have't with saying 'Good morrow.'(III, iii, 115-118)

Greetings constitute the threshold of illocutionary behavior and civility: they have no propositional content and no sincerity condition; they commit the speaker only to being a member of the community whose conventional means of expressing courtesy he is invoking. When Coriolanus refuses even to greet a common citizen, he sets himself completely apart from the community. Thus, when the citizens banish him, they simply ratify what he has already said and done. But Coriolanus must have the final word. So, he delivers his famous declarative: "I banish you" (III, iii, 153). By banishing those who have banished him, Coriolanus "makes explicit his intention to stand alone, as a society of one, as a state complete in himself" and

---

6 All quotations of *Coriolanus* are from the text edited by Louis B. Wright (New York: Washington Square Press, 1974).

"answerable only to the laws he himself promulgates" (Fish, 1001). After his banishment, Coriolanus goes to his old enemy Aufidius and becomes his ally against Rome. Aufidius lets him take command. Coriolanus, like a god, demands absolute obedience to his word, because it is *his*. He promises Aufidius to attack Rome but, in the end, goes back on his pledge. He stands against his own word and "is struck down accordingly" (Fish, 1002).

In *Coriolanus*, individual transgression is clearly set against a context of well established and upheld conventions. In his explicit refusal to honor such conventions, Coriolanus acknowledges their existence and their binding force. In *La Celestina*, on the contrary, individual transgressions are played against an equally transgressive context, where rules and shared procedures are obsessively invoked but none is ever consistently honored or upheld. This duplicity is built in the unusual number of the play's asides, which create a sharp discrepancy between what the characters say to each other and what they acknowledge to themselves and the audience. In the asides, the speaker breaks away from the I-YOU-HERE-NOW conditions of dialogue and treats the listener not as a *you* who shares the *here* and *now* of his discourse, but as an absent *he*. Presence and absence are also exchanged in Celestina's calling upon the devil (act III), where the absent one is made present by the power of the performative words.[7] While performatives create their own truth conditions, asides in *La Celestina* are used to undermine the truth-value of statements, to reveal the speaker's insincerity or to question the linguistic behavior of others.

Speech Act Theory offered me a new set of questions to ask about every sentence in the text. What kind of speech act is being performed? Are all the necessary conditions for each act only implicit in the dialogue situation? Are all of them explicit? Or only some? And if so, which ones, and how, and by whom are they made explicit in every case? To do this with any text longer than a page takes a good deal of patience and some love for detail. I do not think this is a necessary strategy for analyzing a text, but I have found it a rewarding one in the case of *La Celestina*.

Now, except for making love, killing and dying, the story of *La Celestina* is a story of speech acts: Calisto *declares* his love to Melibea; she *rejects* him; Calisto *asks* for Sempronio's help; Sempronio *advises* him to hire Celestina; Pármeno *warns* Calisto against such a deal; Celestina

---

7 For the opposition *presence/absence* and the indexes "I-you-here-now" as marks of the speech event that constitute *presence*, see Emile Benveniste, *Problèmes de linguistique générale*, I (Paris: Gallimard, 1966), pp. 238 ff. For the "conative" function of magic or incantatory utterances, see Roman Jakobson, "Linguistics and Poetics," in Thomas A. Sebeok, ed., *Style in Language* (Cambridge, Massachusetts: The M.I.T. Press, 1960), pp. 355-357.

promises, and so on, up to the final scene of the play, where Pleberio *laments* the destructive power of love and the essential chaos of the world.

Each of the linguistic actions included in the story summarizes a network of specific speech acts presented in the text. In the first scene, for instance, after Calisto's roundabout declaration, Melibea rejects him by performing a sequence of three speech acts:[8]

CALISTO Por cierto los gloriosos santos, que se deleitan en la visión divina, no gozan más que yo agora en el acatamiento tuyo....

MELIBEA ¿Por gran premio tienes éste, Calisto?

CALISTO Téngolo por tanto en verdad que, si Dios me diese en el cielo la silla sobre sus santos, no lo ternía por tanta felicidad.

MELIBEA *Pues aun más igual galardón te daré yo, si perseveras.*

CALISTO ¡Oh bienaventuradas orejas mías, que indignamente tan gran palabra habéis oído!

MELIBEA Mas desaventuradas de que me acabes de oir, porque *la paga será tan fiera, cual [la] merece tu loco atrevimiento.... Vete, vete de ahí, torpe!*

CALISTO Iré como aquél contra quien solamente la adversa fortuna pone su estudio con odio cruel. (I, pp. 46-47)

First, Melibea promises to reward Calisto, eventually, if he persists as a good courtly lover. Then, after Calisto's overjoyed reply, Melibea violently transforms her former promise into a threat to punish him for his daring. And immediately she honors her threat by banishing Calisto from her presence, supposedly forever.[9]

Promises and threats must include a proposition about some future action by the speaker: "I *will give* you a reward," "I *will punish* you without mercy." The standard structure of a threat is conditional: "*If you keep on talking*, I shall leave the room." The usual structure of a

---

[8] All quotations of *La Celestina* are from the text edited by Dorothy S. Severin (Madrid: Alianza Editorial, 1978).

[9] "When the entirety of discourse is analyzed in terms of speech acts as minimal units, it becomes necessary to recognize each sequential unit as complex, as perhaps a bundle of features. It is not enough to place an act as, say, a promise or a threat; one will need to specify a speech act in terms of several functional foci, or several components. Perhaps the minimum number of foci or components needing to be specified will be always at least three. in terms of functional foci, for example, that an act is (referentially) a threat, but (expressively) a mock threat, and (rhetorically, or in contact function within the course of an utterance) also a summons; in terms of components, that an act is in message content (topic), a threat; in key, mock; and in norm of interaction, a summons" (Hymes, p. 53). For the characterization of the different kinds of foci or components of speech acts, see Hymes, pp. 53-62.

promise, on the other hand, is categorical, it has no *if* clause: "I promise I will return your love." In uttering a promise or a threat, the speaker implies that he is able to perform the action in question (*ability* condition) and that he intends to perform it (*sincerity* condition). The utterance of a threat or a promise counts as a commitment to honor with future action the present words. Like all other speech acts, commissives must satisfy the so-called *non-obviousness* condition: it would make no sense, for instance, to promise you something that you and I know I will have to do in any case. Promises and threats have the same set of necessary conditions, except for the one about the listener's interests: in a promise, the future action of the speaker must be something the listener wants the speaker to do; in a threat, that future action must be something damaging to the listener or a least contrary to his wishes.

Melibea's transformation of her initial promise into a threat is prefigured in the formal construction of her utterances: she promises with the conditional structure of a threat ("más igual galardón te daré yo, *si perseveras*) and threatens with the categorical structure of a promise ("la paga será tan fiera, cual la merece tu loco atrevimiento"). The key to this ironic transformation is that both Melibea's promise to reward Calisto and her threat to punish him satisfy their respective necessary conditions with the same specific elements. Melibea's ability to reward and punish depends on where she stands, both personally and institutionally, in relation to Calisto. In his declaration, Calisto invokes the conventions of courtly love and, in doing so, places Melibea in a position of absolute power and authority over him. Since the life of a courtly lover is defined by suffering and endurance, the role of a courtly lady is to respond, initially at least, with deferment or rejection. Thus, Melibea's role makes her promise logically 'non-obvious' and therefore unexpected within the courtly game.

Calisto's yearning for Melibea is made abundantly explicit in his opening address. Melibea's intention to reward him is implicit in her promise. Her sincerity is assumed in Calisto's reply and denied in her ensuing threat. But however insincere her promise may be, its essential condition holds: Melibea has undertaken an obligation to return Calisto's love, if he persists. Only because Melibea's promise counts, can her threat satisfy all the necessary conditions. Melibea's promise changes the rules of the courtly game: by purporting to accept Calisto, she makes rejection no longer expected and therefore non-obvious. This is what gives her threat its overwhelming force.

Melibea's threat is held in all its force by her ensuing command and by Calisto's humble obedience. And because it holds, her threat establishes her "true" intentions and reveals her former promise as deliberately defective. Yet, in spite of such "true" intentions, the plot of *La Celestina* makes Melibea retrace backwards with her actions the path she had drawn forward with her words. In acts I-XI, Calisto persists, through Celestina's mediation. In acts XII-XIX, Melibea rewards Calisto with her illicit love. Melibea's defective promise is thus honored in the development of the plot. And in such honoring, her forceful threat is also ironically revoked. Yet, in turn, her revoked threat is made somberly overreaching, far beyond what Melibea ever intended: the text makes Calisto pay dearly for his daring with public dishonor and death.[10]

Rejection in the form of a threat is not only Melibea's first act, but also her last:

> MELIBEA Padre mío, no pugnes ni trabajes por venir adonde yo estoy, que estorbarás la presente habla que te quiero hacer. Lastimado serás brevemente con la muerte de tu única hija. Mi fin es llegado.... Si me escuchas sin lágrimas, oirás la causa desesperada de mi forzada y alegre partida. No la interrumpas con lloro ni palabras; si no, quedarás más quejoso en no saber por qué me mato, que doloroso por verme muerta. Ninguna cosa me preguntes ni respondas, más de lo que de mi grado decirte quisiere. (XX, p. 229)

In her initial threat to Calisto, Melibea had made her courtly function coincide perfectly with her social role. She had played the unattainable lady by speaking as an honorable young woman, aware of her social identity and responsibilities. Melibea had threatened Calisto with absence and silence. Implicitly present in her initial speech was the figure of the father, to whom she had tacitly pledged her loyalty against Calisto's solicitation. In the first scene, Melibea's self had been clearly defined in terms of social institutions. In her final threat to her father, Melibea speaks as a woman in love, well aware that she has irreparably broken her ties to family and society. She threatens to punish Pleberio's yet unspoken words with a silence which will only accelerate the final silence of her death. Implicitly present in her last speech is the figure of her lover, to whom Melibea pledges symbolic loyalty against her father's solicitude.

Melibea's threat to Pleberio reveals that their old, cherished roles are no longer available. In assuming full responsibility for her transgression—an assumption that can only take place in discourse—Melibea gains over her father a fleeting but absolute authority. And in doing so, she shows the fragility of the institution which used to

---

10 For the inevitable destruction of the courtly lover in a fully developed narrative or dramatic text, see Inés Azar, "Metáfora, literalidad, transgresión: amor-muerte en *La Celestina* y en la *Égloga II* de Garcilaso," *Lexis*, 3 (1979), 57-65.

bind them together. Her own authority is no less frail. True, she has the last words. But this is so, because these are the last words she shall ever have. Melibea's responsibility for her transgression can only be fulfilled in dying, because she has chosen—more radically than Coriolanus—a self with no others. Calisto was for her—as she for him—a confirmation that an enclosed, sufficient, isolated self was still possible. Once she has lost Calisto, Melibea's affirmation of self can only take the paradoxical form of self-destruction.

Promises and threats are unusually frequent in *La Celestina*. They are probably the most important speech acts performed in the play, which is fitting for a work that so obsessively raises the question of speech and responsibility.[11] After all, promises and threats are the only class of speech acts which have as their essential condition the commitment to make our words true *in* our deeds.

Celestina is, of course, the most interesting character in terms of linguistic behavior. She uses words as if she could establish, in every utterance, the world anew. In her mouth, the referential value of statements collapses, the commitment of promises has no lasting effect. She recognizes no institution, yet pays lip service to all of them. Celestina believes herself to be The Institution, the only one.[12] Coriolanus defines himself against social custom. Celestina identifies social custom with her self. Coriolanus rejects. Celestina encompasses. Coriolanus demands that performatives be measured by standards of referential truth they cannot satisfy. Celestina transforms everything she says into a performative, neither true nor false, but in a disturbing sense, one probably never envisioned by Austin.

Celestina's power and authority depend on her ability to manipulate others into accepting her as the institution which establishes procedures and conventions, every time, for every act: she arouses the self-interest of others and lures them into believing that, if they do as she says, she will get them what they want. In fact, Celestina chooses for them the objects of their desire. And she

---

11 On the question of language and discourse in the text and in the world of *La Celestina*, see Malcolm K. Read, "*La Celestina* and the Renaissance Philosophy of Language," *Philological Quarterly*, 55 (1976), 166-177, and "Fernando de Rojas' Vision of the Birth and the Death of Language," *MLN*, 93 (1978), 163-175.

12 Celestina's institutional character is not simply a matter of *her* beliefs: "In their [the characters'] community, the testimony of Rojas's text indicates clearly, Celestina is an institution more central and vital than the Church (repository of that other, archaic Authority), more adored for her miracles and mediation than its saints, and more sought after, even in church and on holy occasions, than its clerics" (George A. Shipley, "Authority and Experience in *la Celestina*," *Bulletin of Hispanic Studies*, 62 [1985], 98).

chooses only those objects that she knows she can eventually deliver. Yet, by giving her the gold chain, Calisto unwittingly chooses for Pármeno and Sempronio a new object of desire and for Celestina a prize that she will never relinquish. When the self-interest of Pármeno and Sempronio can no longer be reconciled with her own, Celestina's "institutional" power ceases to exist. Like anyone else, she is now accountable for her past commitments. She can no longer undo them. What brings her final downfall is that, unlike any other institution, Celestina has only her words to constitute her acts and the self-interest of others to confirm their value. No lasting institution is based purely on verbal behavior or sustained exclusively by selfishness.

In *La Celestina*—as in *Coriolanus*—the plot is the unfolding of linguistic behavior and its necessary consequences. Yet, no single character, not even Celestina, can account for the entire course of action in the play. What unfolds in the tragi-comedy is not a line, but a network of interrelated acts, performed by interrelated characters, who produce with their actions a network of interrelated consequences. The final irony of the play is that the unfolding of so well tied a structure shatters all pre-existing ties: at the end, servants are left without master, parents without child, society without its institutional continuity.

Both *Coriolanus* and *La Celestina* raise the question of personal identity and definition of self against the background of social intercourse, identity and roles. The autonomous self that Coriolanus proclaims, Melibea demands, Celestina briefly enjoys, can only be relative and must be borrowed from the model of social institutions. In this sense, Coriolanus is an exemplary case: by becoming a law unto himself, he is not freed from the burden of social conventions; on the contrary, he unintentionally reveals their inevitability. His defiant assertion of self consists of the same gestures he purports to reject: after his banishment, his promises, requests and commands are what they are, not because Coriolanus utters them, but because in uttering them he uses now the communal words, in their prescribed contexts, with their conventional meanings, values and effects. Shakespeare's play presents a view that could be articulated, and obviously was, long before Speech Act Theory came into existence: for a truly autonomous self there is no name, because there is no society; no reference, because there is nothing "other" to refer to; no "I," because there is no "you"; no speech, no language:

Coriolanus
He would not answer to; forbade all names;
He was a kind of nothing, titleless. (V, i, 12-14)

This is also the view that *La Celestina* presents in its most extreme, negative formulation.

Fish warns against generalizing applications such as his to all literary texts. He also warns, with reason, against trying to make Speech Act theory become a theory of literary criticism. But Fish goes on to suggest that the theory can do something with literary texts only if the texts prefigure the theory, which—he thinks—very few do; Coriolanus happens to be a happy exception. I do not agree with Fish in his all-out restrictions. True, Speech Act Theory cannot do everything for the critic, but it can do more than Fish is willing to admit. It can be used, fruitfully, I think, to analyze sincerity and lying, duplicity, misunderstanding, responsibility, authority and power manipulations in any given discourse. It can also be applied to some specific literary questions, such as the reliability of narrative voices or the characterization of courtly love, for instance, as a code or system of speech acts. The theory is obviously fitted to the study of dialogue and more specifically to the analysis of drama, since dramatic action is constituted by linguistic events and the fate of dramatic characters depends significantly on their linguistic behavior.[13]

Speech Act Theory makes explicit what the speakers of any community know implicitly just because they are speakers: that there are some shared and binding conventions which create intelligibility and therefore make communication possible.[14] Intelligibility is assumed, but it is not a pre-existing concept on which the theory is built, it is its object. The theory does not explain *why* we can or do communicate, but *how* we do it: not *with*, or *by means of*, but *in* those shared and binding conventions which create our institutions and *are* our intelligibility.

What the theory offers is a descriptive language with conventional meanings, values and effects with which we can agree to talk "responsibly" about discourse in *La Celestina*, in *Coriolanus*, in other texts or in daily life. To assume responsibility for analyzing discourse with the descriptive tools of Speech Act Theory is not inconsequential. The theory holds, both implicitly and explicitly, some definite views on such well-known dichotomies as self/others, words/deeds, authority/responsibility. Speech is not opposed to action, it is a form of action. Authority does not necessarily give rise to responsibility; on the contrary, by assuming responsibility—even by not assuming it when we should—we create authority. Self is a function of others, because it exists in discourse, which we can appropriate, but only at the price of submitting to pre-existing conventions. Responsibility is

---

[13] Cf. Keir Elam, *The Semiotics of Theatre and Drama* (London and New York: Methuen, 1980), pp. 156-176.

[14] "From the standpoint of the ethnography of speaking, there is in a community a system of speech acts, a structured knowledge accessible to the members of the community, and so, to a great extent, to science" (Hymes, p. 102).

impossible within a totally autonomous self; it exists in the transaction between self and others. Only metaphorically and on the basis of the *I-you* transaction can I make myself responsible to myself. Shared and binding conventions constitute not only language but all institutions. Speech Act Theory commits its users to an institutionalist view, not necessarily of human nature, but certainly of human behavior.[15]

George Washington University

[15] For an account that finds the power of Speech Act Theory precisely in its insistence on socially upheld conventions and accepted practices, see Sandy Petrey, "Speech Acts in Society: Fish, Felman, Austin and God," *Texte*, 3 (1984): 43-61. For an account that also credits Speech Act Theory with having placed language in its social context but argues that the theory has been so far unable to characterize discourse as a social practice, see Mary Louise Pratt, "The Ideology of Speech-Act Theory," *Centrum* New Series, 1 (1981), 5-18.

Strategies of Ambiguity:
The Honor Conflict in
La batalla del honor

MARGARET R. HICKS

N THE HIGHLY CONVENTIONALIZED WORLD of Lope's theater, conflicts of honor tend to conform to a recognizable pattern characterized by numerous variables. Conspicuous among those features differing from play to play, and thus allowing for the circumstantiality of a given plot, are the particular strategies adopted by the opponents. Where violence in the cause of honor is either forbidden or at least to be avoided, the implementation of such offensive and defensive tactics becomes a dominant structural feature of the play.

Typically, the protagonist is made aware of the threat to his honor only to recognize his inability to act openly and in the prescribed manner. The complications giving rise to this situation are subject to considerable variation of detail, but a characteristic feature is the issue of hierarchy. Because his adversary is a figure of higher rank or greater authority, the protagonist is forbidden the conventional response of open challenge and the consequent drawing of swords. Rather, he is obliged to pursue a policy of subversion, of indirect attack; or to put it another way, his defensive tactics must of necessity incorporate a degree of cunning and artifice.

The protagonist in *La batalla del honor* is placed in just such a position. Although Carlos is himself a nobleman of high rank, his adversary is none other than the king. Denied the right to challenge this powerful enemy and mindful of the need to conceal from public knowledge the threat to his honor, Carlos is forced to rely on subterfuge. His defensive maneuvers are notable for their depen-

dence on the subtle use of language to express indirectly and in
ambiguous terms the warnings and challenges that cannot be declared
openly. One of Lope's earlier plays, *La batalla del honor* has received little
critical attention, although several good editions are available. I will
use the most recent edition, prepared by Henryk Ziomek and based
on Lope's autograph play, dated 1608.

In his important study of Lope's honor plays, Donald Larson
dismisses *La batalla del honor* on the grounds that the dramatic interest
of the play centers on feminine virtue rather than on the purely
masculine values embodied in the code of honor (171). The protagonist's wife is indeed a paragon of virtue and loyalty, and her role is
significant for that very reason. But I would argue that the focus of
dramatic interest is rather upon the battle of wits waged between the
hero and his adversary. The bizarre plots concocted by the king and
the protagonist's desperate counterplots together comprise the action
of the play. Were it not for the demands of the code of honor, such
plots and counterplots would clearly be unnecessary, even pointless.

The antagonist in this play is not an entirely unsympathetic
figure. Introduced in the first scene as a very young king only
recently ascended to the throne, he is chided by his adviser for failing
to curb his desire for the unobtainable Blanca. Henrique reminds him
that in pursuing Carlos' wife, the king is ignoring, indeed flouting, his
obligations to a loyal vassal. Pleas for reason and restraint are to no
avail, however, for the king has chosen to follow the dictates of his
passion:

> Blanca, en quien la mano franca,
> de naturaleza bella,
>   tan liberal se ha mostrado,
> yo os amo con tal passion
> que el discurso de razon
> habeys al alma quitado.
>   (I, 71-76)

The initial impression of youthful irresponsibility is echoed by Carlos
himself in the following scene, as he laments the invidiousness of his
own position:

> Çielos, ¿que es lo que procuro,
> viendo mis çelos tan claros?
>   No por la parte que toca
> a Blanca, mi esposa amada,
> porque estara, conquistada,
> como en la mar firme roca;
> mas por la parte de el rey,
> mançebo, aunque onesto y sabio,

dispuesto a mi ynjusto agrabio,
porque Amor es rey sin ley.
(I, 103-112)

The conventional social contract between lord and vassal is repeatedly violated by the king as he persists in his attempts to seduce Blanca. Carlos, for his part, is placed in an impossible predicament. He must act in order to preserve his honor, yet he is restricted by the terms of the social contract and unwilling to overstep the bounds of his own authority. There exists a procedure for warning and challenging according to the code of honor, and the physical act of drawing swords is a necessary corollary to the verbal challenge. Obviously, the vassal who initiates such a procedure against his king faces dire consequences. Even in the middle of the second act, when the need for action is ever more imperative, Carlos continues to reject any thought of open defiance of the king's authority:

> De su amor
> estoy çierto; que mi honor
> es el que batalla agora
>   con el poder de un tirano.
> ¿Tirano? Eso no, xamas;
> de mi honor, si; en lo demas
> es mi señor soberano.
>   (II, 1346-1352)

Carlos becomes increasingly apprehensive of the threat of dishonor in the course of the play. He dare not challenge his adversary and, indeed, any sort of direct confrontation could lead only to public discovery of the affront to his honor. Unwilling to violate the conventions of his social code, Carlos rather freely violates a different set of conventions in his various attempts to countermine the king's plots. In the interest of secrecy and decorum, he undertakes the use of metaphor, irony and ambiguity to "implicate" what he cannot state openly and directly.

The field of speech-act theory offers a convenient perspective from which to analyse this use of language as stratagem. Particularly appropriate here is Neal R. Norrick's identification of the double bind situation as an important source of nondirect speech acts (33-46). Acknowledging his indebtedness to H. P. Grice's discussion of conversational implicature in "Logic and Conversation," he further develops Grice's notion of maxim conflict. The double bind, according to Norrick, is the result of a conflict between conversational maxims (the conventions governing verbal communication in a given language community) and nonconversational maxims (the conventions governing other aspects of behavior in that community). An individual is forced to choose between the two sets of conventions if, for example, a social taboo conflicts with, say, speaking the truth or even with speaking clearly and to the point. If he defers to the social convention, the individual must then break with one or more of the conversational maxims, either engaging in nondirect speech or simply refusing to speak at all. Moreover, figurative language, or language in which the implied meaning is distinct from the literal, is a major category of nondirect speech acts. The individual caught in the double bind may thus choose to speak metaphorically or ambiguously in order to avoid violating the social convention.

Double bind, then, is an apt description of Carlos' predicament. To speak openly would be to publicize the affront to his honor; to speak directly to the king would imply a challenge that he is neither willing nor entitled to make. By the middle of the second act, however, he has embarked upon a course of indirect warning and veiled reproof that will eventually take effect and touch the conscience of the king.

Having dealt successfully with the king's attempt to suborn his servants, Carlos is confronted by another scheme to install a go-between in his house. The king's ploy is to honor him with the title of *cazador mayor* while insisting that he accept a live-in adviser, a skilled huntsman named Teodoro. Recognizing the dubious tribute as a veritable Trojan horse, Carlos manages to convey a message incorporating censure and warning under the guise of courteous acknowledgement. Making ironic reference to the king's unseemly behavior, Carlos commissions Teodoro to present his homage and his gift to the young monarch:

> no se que dar a su alteza;
> mas, pues es mozo y galan,
> y anda de noche, y le dan
> ocasion graçia y belleza
>   de alguna mujer dichosa
> para andar a cuchilladas
> yo tengo buenas espadas;
> darele la mas famosa
>   y una rodela que creo
> que no passe una pistola
> lo que es la cubierta sola.
> Esto es mostrar mi desseo.
>   (II, 1561-72)

The gift itself bears a warning couched in symbolic terms. The sword is accompanied by a shield bearing a painted figure and a motto. The figure represented is an angel standing at the gates of paradise and holding aloft a flaming sword. The motto is a Latin inscription, *Custos honoris*, guardian of honor. The king's reaction upon examining the shield leaves no doubt that he has indeed understood the meaning: "Si no es maliçia, es aviso." (1736) That which the protagonist cannot say directly to the king, he can imply to the messenger, Teodoro, or place in the mouth of a higher authority. Voicing his fear of returning to Carlos' house, Teodoro indicates that he too has understood the warning implicit in the emblem:

> Pues si un angel para ti
> muestra una espada, ¿que hara
> para mi Carlos, que ya
> tiene sospechas de mi?
> (II, 1741-44)

This stratagem, for all its ingenuity, does not bring about the desired effect. Far from taking heed, the young king angrily resolves to wage a frontal attack, reminding Teodoro that he, after all, possesses the advantages of authority and power.

From this point on, husband and wife find themselves virtually subjected to a state of siege. Insisting, ironically, that Carlos is suspected of hatching plots against the crown, the king convinces neighbors of the need to spy on his household. He succeeds in having sections of the connecting walls blown away so that he may gain access to Blanca more easily. To account for the absurdity of this rather bizarre scheme, one could cite the numerous references to the king's abnormal state of mind. Consistently ignoring the advice and even the rebukes of his advisers, he freely admits that his actions are not rational. His repeated admissions of *locura* are echoed by the courtiers themselves as they attempt to turn him from his folly. When he first announces his intention to carry out "una amorosa fuerza vengativa" (II, 1781), for instance, Henrique openly accuses him of madness: "Ya te priva/del seso la pasion." (1782-83)

Carlos, for his part, has become doubly cautious and more determined to rely on his own devices. Having forced the hapless Teodoro to admit to his appointed role as spy and pander, he sends the man away with a warning. Confident that he has won a small victory, he resolves to keep his own counsel, trusting in his ability to keep the king at bay:

> Y a la espia que prendi
> en la batalla de honor
> buelbo a soltar que es mexor;
> pues su desinio entendi,
>   segura esta la victoria;
> corazon, ya no ay que temas,
> pues que las estratagemas
> se han de bolver en tu gloria.
> (II, 1864-71)

This resolution is put to the test near the end of the second act. About to enter his garden, Carlos is startled to hear the voice of the king addressing Blanca. Conscious of the fact that his enemy is at this moment at his mercy, he nonetheless checks his impulse to violence acknowledging his obligations as a subject:

> Tentandome esta la yra,
> y enfrenando la lealtad;
> matarle es cruel maldad;
> Dios en su ymagen se mira.
> (II, 1984-87)

Determined to outmaneuver his adversary, Carlos calls out to warn of his approach, thereby allowing time for the king to conceal himself. Aware that his enemy is nearby and listening, he proceeds to praise Blanca for her fidelity and to issue an oblique warning to the king:

> ¡Vive Dios! que de manera
> te adoro y asi me ynprime
> amor tu virtud, que creo
> que quando fuesse posible
> que el mismo rey te sirbiesse,
> que nunca los reyes sirben
> las mugeres de sus deudos,
> mayormente los que siguen
> los passos de sus mayores,
> y mas donde es bien que ymiten
> tantos Carlos y Luises,
> que creo, que le matasse.
> (II, 2048-59)

The next test of Carlos' skill as a strategist occurs near the beginning of the third act. Unable to restrain his passion, the king once again enters through the broken wall in search of Blanca. On this occasion he finds her sleeping in the garden, seemingly alone. Ever on guard, however, Carlos is sitting in the shadows nearby. Speaking to the still sleeping figure and announcing his intention to embrace her, the king is arrested by a voice from the shadows: "No hagas tal." (2293) Confused by the repetition of this warning, he concludes that the voice must in reality be that of his conscience:

> "¡No hagas tal!" "¡Miralo bien!"
> ¿No es eco de mi razon?
> Causado me ha confusion
> y elado el alma tanbien.
> (III, 2304-07)

Not satisfied with this explanation, he then decides that it must have been someone outside the garden. Not until the speaker still hidden in the shadows identifies himself as Blanca's husband, does the king become really alarmed. Finally stumbling on the truth of the matter, he resolves to withdraw rather than force a confrontation that could have grave consequences:

> ¡Caso estraño! Alli he sentido
> la voz; pues verelo. ¡Ay, çielos,
> o lo ha fingido de çelos,
> o duerme aqui su marido!
> Si durmiera no pudiera
> responder, aunque soñara;
> a proposito, y es clara
> razon, que me oyo y que espera
> a que me baya, avisado
> por respeto que me tiene.
> Yrme y perder me conviene
> la ocassion que Amor me ha dado.
> No quiero andar descubierto
> con hombre tan bien naçido;
> que quien me avisa dormido
> me sabra matar despierto.
> (III, 2316-31)

The king's penetration of Carlos' ruse and his response to the implied threat serve to reinforce the protagonist's confidence in his own ability as a strategist:

> Ya para nuestra batalla
> pues se esta el rey en su tema,
> fue notable estratagema,
> fingiendo sueño, avisalla.
> (III, 2380-83)

Realizing that he must anticipate the king's next move, he advises his wife to give up the elegant dress, jewels and perfumes that she usually wears. Blanca unadorned, he reasons, will be less likely to arouse the king's ardor. As Carlos has foreseen, the king does return uninvited, though with courtiers in attendance to deter any rash action on the part of his reluctant host. What Carlos has not anticipated is the young monarch's vehement reaction to the change in Blanca's appearance. Seizing this opportunity to discredit her husband, the king pretends to interpret her simple attire as an instance of maltreatment. Insisting on the respect due her as his own kinswoman, he announces his intention to effect a divorce.

Confronted with this final threat of defeat, Carlos is mute with
dismay. Interpreting his continued silence as evidence of despair, the
sometime spy, Teodoro, attempts to rally his will to resist. Having
become a partisan of the beleaguered protagonist, Teodoro enjoins
him to give battle and fight for his honor, thus echoing the metaphor
introduced by Carlos himself in the first act and repeated throughout
the play:

> Todavia
> pienso que duermes y sueñas.
> Recuerda, Carlos, que vienen
> los enemigos tan çerca
> que por esa torre Blanca
> buscan de tu honor la puerta.
> ¿No sientes el son del arma?
>   (III, 2578-84)

Carlos responds to Teodoro's call to arms by casting off his clothes
and then proceeding to dramatize the battle metaphor. Teodoro,
never privy to Carlos' strategies, accepts these actions at face value.
He interprets the initial gesture as a sign of mental aberration,
concluding that the subsequent behavior is further proof of madness.
In spite of Carlos' apparent agitation, however, there is evidence that
this mad scene is in fact a performance contrived for Teodoro's
benefit. The first clue is the protagonist's explanation for having torn
off his clothes:

> ¿Nunca has visto en la carrera
> del mar, ençender el fuego
> en una nabe flamenca,
> que las caxas ençendidas,
> joyas, paños, sedas, telas,
> van arrojando a la mar
> porque ellas solas se pierdan?
>   . . . .
> Pues eso mismo hago yo
> porque el alma no se ençienda.
>   (III, 2591-97; 2602-03)

He implies that his apparent repudiation of reason is a conscious ploy,
a final attempt to save himself from disaster. Carlos has chosen to
cast off the merely superficial, the semblance of sanity, in order to
preserve the essential, his identity as a man of honor. To be pitied as
a madman is less odious, presumably, than to be despised as a man
without honor.

His ironic greeting of Teodoro in the next-to-last scene of the play
provides another clue that the mad scene has been a contrivance;

> De los assaltos passados
> me libre, Teodor, tanbien.
> ¿Sanaste de aquel balazo?
> (III, 3010-12)

This boast of victory in the last skirmish is another ambiguous
statement. On the surface, of course, it reflects the madman's preoccupation with his *tema*; but it also recalls the protagonist's earlier
assertions of confidence after a successful encounter with his adversary. It appears to be an ironical version of "notable estratagema," in
fact. Recognizing that the man is, after all, still subject to the king's
bidding, Carlos has never trusted or confided in the sympathetic
Teodoro. Considered in the light of his distrust, this greeting is surely
a sardonic reference to a successful deception.

Finally, the extension and dramatization of the battle metaphor is
not confined to this mad scene. The elaboration of the metaphor here
is rather the culmination of a process begun earlier in the play.
Having introduced the battle image at the end of the first act, Carlos
thereafter makes repeated references to his "batalla del honor." He
frequently expands the allusion with details that impart a decidedly
allegorical flavor. For instance, after discovering the treachery of his
servants early in the second act, he laments his predicament in terms
that recall the device of the psychomachia:

> Todo soy batalla en mi;
> mas como el onor batalla
> contra el poder, sufre y calla
> la razon que ya perdi.
> Por alli viene un soldado
> que a la venganza me anima,
> otro por alli que estima
> la lealtad que le he jurado.
> (II, 1229-36)

In the opening scene of the third act, Carlos again alludes to his plight
in allegorical terms:

> La mina se ha descubierto,
> y el portillo del conçierto
> que dava al rey puerta franca;
> a saber voy, torre blanca,
> si algun soldado me han muerto.
> (III, 2136-40)

It is this very allegorical quality that characterizes his fiction of
locura. Although Carlos is identified throughout the play as a military
figure, the *Almirante*, his role in this mad scene does not call up the

image of a commander in an actual battle. Rather, his performance is
self-consciously literary in tone, and he more closely resembles the
narrator of a medieval allegory. As Henryk Ziomek points out in his
introduction to the play, the allegorical features of this scene are
reminiscent of the battle between Doña Cuaresma and Don Carnal in
the *Libro de buen amor* (24). The scene is rather a long one, but the
following excerpt will suffice to illustrate its allegorical character;

> TEODORO
> ALMIRANTE
>   ¡Brabos soldados!
> El mismo honor los engendra.
> De las vanderas de guardia
> va formando las yleras,
> y luego las compañias
> que van suçediendo a estas,
> y aguarneçe el esquadron
> de quatro mangas tudescas
> de arcabuzes, de suspiros
> que las esquinas rodean.
> Ya da el orden; y la fama,
> a tambor mayor, comienza
> a deçir que se recojan
> para marchar mas apriessa;
> ya el capitan de canpaña
> llamado Onrrosa Defensa,
> haze cargar el bagaje
> de pensamientos y penas.
> Por vanguardia va delante
> la ymaginaçion ligera,
> las vanderas en el çentro
> del esquadron todas negras...
>   (III, 2674-95)

This is actually the first of two mad scenes, the second occuring
near the end of the third act. If the former scene is distinguished by
its allegorical tone, the latter is characterized by a strong note of self-
conscious irony that serves to heighten the impression of calculation
and artifice. Carlos appears onstage accompanied by his servants,
Leonelo and Dionis, who are attempting to restrain him both physi-
cally and with pleas for rational conduct. Recalling the incident of the
unfaithful servants in the second act, Carlos turns against the two
retainers and, in oblique terms, challenges their loyalty. Retreating
behind a fiction, he identifies himself with the unfortunate Actaeon,
transformed by Diana into a stag and subsequently savaged by his

own dogs. Pretending to rail against the ungrateful animals, he is
clearly aiming his accusations at the two servants:

> Oyd los perros ladrar.
> Traydores ¿no conozeys
> el pan que os solia dar?
> ¿A vuestro dueño quereys
> despedazar y matar?
> Ten esse alano, Leonelo.
> Ten esse lebrel, Dionis.
> ¡Que me muerde! ¡Ayuda, çielo!
> (III, 2932-39)

Proceeding with this fiction, Carlos requests a mirror so that he
may view the physical manifestation of his dishonor. With obvious
reference to the stag's horns, he thus dramatizes the repugnancy of
his position: "¿Este pellejo/no muestra mi desonor?" (2942-43) As if
to underline the meaning of his veiled rebuke, Carlos accepts the
mirror, turning the glass toward the servants and posing another
rhetorical question with ironical overtones: "¿Los amigos tienen ya/
las caras, Leonelo, ansi?" (2950-51)

The servants, however, show no sign of having grasped the
implications of this outburst. Acknowledging only the literal meaning
of the words, Leonelo attempts in the first instance to assure Carlos
that he is a man and not a stag; later he simply instructs his master to
reverse the mirror. The servants' failure to recognize the intended
implicature is linked to their assumptions about Carlos' state of mind.
Having exhibited irrational behavior in the earlier scene, he is consequently judged incapable of rational discourse. The implications of his
speech in this scene—fairly obvious to the detached observer—are not
accessible to the servants precisely because they expect to hear
nothing but the ravings of a madman.

The protagonist's manipulation of language in the two mad scenes
is not essentially different from his use of figurative or ambiguous
language elsewhere in the play. Even his identification with Actaeon
is introduced in terms of a comparison so that the effect of his
performance is one of self-conscious play-acting. Having acknowledged that, in the final analysis, he is powerless against the authority
of the king, Carlos insists that his overwrought imagination is increasing his suffering. Apparently agreeing with Leonelo's argument
that the creations of the imagination should never be confused with
reality, he proceeds to imagine himself in the role of Actaeon:

> En razon
> esse argumento has fundado.
> Pero ¿sabeys que ymagino

> que soy Anteon, que vi
> de Diana el cristalino
> cuerpo, y que me converti
> en çierbo?
>   (III, 2925-31)

Carlos appropriates this fiction in order to dramatize his own predicament. Calling into question even the loyalty of trusted servants,
he again voices his fear of the ubiquity and the corruptive influence
of royal power.

What actually distinguishes the use of language in these two
scenes is the fact that the protagonist's words are circumscribed by
his violent and seemingly unrestrained actions. Carlos has identified
himself as a man in the grip of unreason and is, therefore, assumed to
have rejected the conventions of speech that obtain among the
normal, sane members of his community. By feigning madness, he
has suspended the basic "conditions of intelligibility" that make effective communication possible (Fish, 1024). The implications of his
ambiguous statements, comprehensible to the reader, thus remain
unintelligible to his audience within the play.

The preoccupation with Carlos' erratic behavior at the expense of
his speech is best illustrated in Teodoro's report to the king following
the first mad scene. Attempting to inspire pity for the protagonist's
plight, Teodoro glosses over the dramatization of the battle of honor
to focus instead on the physical manifestations of lunacy exhibited by
Carlos:

> Luego que de su casa te partiste
> del almirante Carlos, con proposito
> de hazer que por justicia se apartassen,
> tal ymaginaçion cayo en su alma,
> llanto en sus ojos, fuego en sus sentidos,
> que comenzo a dar vozes como loco;
> desnudose furioso los vestidos,
> y ultimamente en un estanque, el triste
> de aquel jardin precipitarse quiso.
>   (III, 2850-58)

It is this report, with its emphasis on irrational actions, that finally
touches the king's conscience. Convinced that he is responsible for
Carlos' pitiable condition, his reaction is immediate. Repenting of his
own *locura* and vowing to redress the wrong, the king announces his
intention to marry the protagonist's sister.

The most compelling and effective rebuke of the king's folly is
thus communicated through the fiction of Carlos' madness. His previous stratagems, effective only in the short term, have been charac-

terized by the use of subtle, nondirect speech. There is intentional ambiguity, but no intention to deceive. The king is meant to see through the window-dressing of the gifts and of Carlos' pretense of talking in his sleep. On the other hand, the king is not meant to penetrate the fiction of madness. Even Carlos' speech contributes to the illusion of *locura* to the extent that the other characters must interpret it in the light of his bizarre actions. Figurative language, ambiguity and irony are therefore reduced to the level of unintelligible nonsense.

Madness, feigned or real, precludes the possibility of effective verbal communication because the madman, even the *loco fingido*, has opted out or repudiated the conventions that make rational discourse possible. He has, in effect, stepped outside the bounds of his community and has placed himself beyond the pale. His position is much like that of the dishonored man, but with one very important distinction: his reintegration into the community does not depend upon the bloody sword of vengeance.

In this play, the stratagem of feigned madness is the vehicle by which the protagonist escapes the ignominy of dishonor and reclaims his place in the social order. Like the painted emblem on the shield, the figure of mad Carlos is an effective though nondirect means of rebuking the king for his transgressions and reminding him of his own *locura*. Precisely because Carlos is a man and not a mere emblematic figure, however, this message has the power to elicit the king's pity and to shame him into recalling his obligations to a loyal vassal.

DUQUESNE UNIVERSITY

Works Cited

Fish, Stanley E. "How to Do Things With Austin and Searle: Speech Act Theory and literary Criticism." *MLN* 91 (1976): 983-1025

Grice, H. Paul. "Logic and Conversation." In Peter Cole and Jerry Morgan, *Syntax and Semantics* 3. *Speech Acts*. NY: Academic Press, 1972, 41-58.

Larson, Donald R. *The Honor Play of Lope de Vega*. Cambridge: Harvard University Press, 1977.

Norrick, Neal R. "Nondirect Speech Acts and Double Binds." *Poetics* 10 (1980): 33-47.

Vega Carpio, Lope de. *La batalla del honor*. Ed. Henryk Ziomek. Athens: University of Georgia Press, 1972.

"Yo quiero hablar claro": Language as the Motivating Force of Lope's *La dama boba*

Catherine Larson

N TWO KEY MOMENTS of Lope's *La dama boba*, the principal characters refer directly to language as they grapple with the problems of awakening to love and to their inner selves. The intelligent sister, Nise, cries, "Yo quiero hablar claro," while she desperately seeks to regain control of the course of the dramatic action. Her formerly simple sister, Finea, describes her own transformation by means of an image which underscores the communicative act: she tells her lover, "Por hablarte supe hablar." These examples of Lope's interest in language and in communication are merely representative of the large number of self-conscious references to language in *La dama boba*; a close examination of these linguistically-oriented elements suggests a self-referential substructure for the play, in which language and its transforming power become the focus of attention.

A linguistic approach to this play is hardly revolutionary; indeed, it offers a reading which complements earlier interpretations of the comedy. Critical attention with respect to *La dama boba* has traditionally centered upon studies of its rich imagery, its underlying philosophical bases, and its strength as a comic work.[1] All these

---

[1] See Donald R. Larson, "*La dama boba* and the Comic Sense of Life," *Romanische Forschungen*, 85 (1973), 41-62; Robert ter Horst, "The True Mind of Marriage: Ironies of the Intellect in Lope's *La dama boba*," *Romanistisches Jahrbuch*, 27 (1976), 347-63; Ronald E. Surtz, "Daughter of Night, Daughter of Light: The Imagery of Finea's Transformation in *La dama boba*," *Bulletin of the Comediantes*, 13, No. 2 (Fall 1961), 1-3; and James E. Holloway, "Lope's Neoplatonism: *La dama boba*," *Bulletin of Hispanic Studies*, 49 (1972), 236-55.

studies have attested to the play's success through the years and to its validity as a powerful work of art. As James Holloway affirms, *La dama boba* reflects "Lope's view of reality given form in poetry, in action, in characterization."[2] Yet, as noted above, the play operates on another level, as well. It is a dramatic text which foregrounds language; it not only deals with language in the ways that all plays deal with language, but also exhibits even deeper levels of communication, self-consciously calling attention to itself as drama and as linguistically-constructed art. An exploration of these self-conscious attempts to communicate can thus expose an underlying structure—and an underlying message for the reader / spectator.

In a recent article on *El castigo sin venganza*, Melveena McKendrick explored the link between the play's language and its inner ambiguity:

> The play seems... to reveal clearly that Lope, long before the advent of linguistic theory and philosophy, was aware of the creative and manipulative functions of language and aware, too, that non-truth and less-than-truth is a primary part of this function. Language has an infinite capacity to misinform, conceal, invent, leave ambiguous, and mislead... The main function of speech is rarely that of straightforward communication, and Lope knew it.[3]

Language in *La dama boba* functions in much the same way that McKendrick has described in *El castigo sin venganza*. The play continually underscores linguistic manipulation—both in its ordinary, "everyday" use as dialogue and in its metaliterary and extratextual references. Lope alters the dramatic world created onstage through the power of language, language which is employed quite differently by the two sisters, Finea and Nise. Throughout much of the play, Finea is a simpleton, while her sister is well-educated and highly sophisticated. The sisters' two principal suitors, Liseo and Laurencio, also presented as opposing characters, are primarily contrasted through their reactions to Finea's boorish behavior. The dualities seen in these two sets of characters are revealed through their uses and abuses of language, for in *La dama boba*, words make the man or woman. What happens to each character in the final scene of the play is more a function of what they say and how they say it than of what they do or how they do it. Language—or, even more specifically, language *as* action—becomes the ultimate determinant of each character's fate.

To understand how language becomes the determining factor in the play's resolution, we must understand how the two sisters' use of language is turned upside down in the course of the play. Nise is

---

[2] Holloway, p. 239.

[3] Melveena McKendrick, "Language and Silence in *El castigo sin venganza*," *Bulletin of the Comediantes*, 35, No. 1 (Summer 1983), p. 83.

intelligent, although at times both arrogant and pedantic. She presents herself as an authority on literature; as literary critic, she comments upon drama, prose, and poetry, even to the point of alluding to a certain Lope de Vega. Yet, by discussing the act of literary creation within the world of another literary work, the dramatic text, Nise constantly reminds us of the intimate relationship between language and art. Her literary lectures thus subtly underscore language's transforming power. They serve as self-conscious reminders that words are the media that writers use to create dramatic texts. Keir Elam notes,"In the drama, the metalinguistic function often has the effect of foregrounding language as object or event by bringing it explicitly to the audience's attention."[4] As readers or spectators of the play, we consequently become increasingly aware of language and of its creative function in art. When characters in a dramatic text talk about literature, and when words remind us about how language functions, we begin to focus upon the relationship between language and the creation of a literary text.

One further note concerning Nise's type of linguistic manipulation merits our attention. Nise frequently fails to take her listeners into account, often talking down to them. She thus reveals herself to be a character who abuses the conventions that are followed by persons (or characters within a mimetic literary text) who really want to communicate.

A key example of this aspect of Nise's characterization is the scene where she meets with several suitors in a literary "academy," discussing literature and critiquing one of the men's original sonnets. The sonnet functions in much the same way as other literary texts that are examined in the play. It displays language by illuminating the ways that language transforms reality in artistic creations.Here, however, the literary creation falls on its face—at least for Nise. The sonnet is so unclear to her that Nise's only response is that the poem was obscure and affected; she exclaims, "Ni una palabra entendí."[5] Although the poet, Duardo, explicates his poem for her, Nise remains arrogantly and adamantly critical: "No discurras, por tu vida;/vete a escuelas" (I. vii. 575-6). Nise, the pseudo-intellectual, has failed to fully comprehend the manipulation of artistic language by another "intellectual," remaining convinced that Duardo is incapable of controlling that language well. She maintains her own pretentious manipulation of language and literary criticism in this early part of the play, but gradually becomes less sure of herself as the comedy

---

    4 Keir Elam, *The Semiotics of Theatre and Drama* (London: Methuen, 1980), p. 156.
    5 Lope de Vega, *La dama boba*, 5th ed., ed. Diego Marín (Madrid: Cátedra, 1981), p. 85 (I. vii. 539). All subsequent citations will be indicated by act, scene, and verse numbers within the text.

progresses and as she is supplanted in the role of linguistic mistress by her sister, Finea.

Finea, the *dama boba,* begins the play as a total simpleton. Ronald Surtz explains her linguistic role: "In the verbal world of the *comedia, bobería* is manifested above all as a failure to grasp symbolic language. Finea interprets literally words and expressions that are used in a figurative sense."[6] Her understanding of how language functions is thus ingenuous in the extreme. Finea's language patterns are illuminated in her school lesson on the alphabet:

> RUFINO. Di aquí: *b, a, n: ban.*
> FINEA. ¿Dónde van?
> ¿Que se van, no me decías?
> RUFINO. Letras son; ¡míralas bien!
> FINEA. Ya miro.
> RUFINO.   *B, e, n: ben.*
> FINEA. ¿Adónde?
> RUFINO.   ¡Adónde en mis días
> no te vuelva más a ver!
> FINEA. ¿Ven, no me dices? Pues ya voy.
> (I. vi. 336-46)

This speech offers a striking example of how dramatic language can be used for characterization. It also utilizes language as its own referent; by focussing upon a lesson on words, the scene foregrounds language as object, accentuating the theme of learning the language of love and tying the use of words to the central structure of the play. Finea begins to learn about how both love and language function in this act; the self-referential lesson on the alphabet focusses our attention on the process of learning. We may then connect Finea's school lesson to the play as a whole—and to the relationship between the play and the reader/spectator. Although the other characters onstage react negatively to her linguistic naiveté, Finea's failures to understand and to communicate are wholly felicitous for the audience.[7] We are simultaneously able to laugh at her linguistic misfirings and see how language affects and effects characterization, while we are subtly reminded of the important role that language

---

    6 Surtz, p. 163.
    7 For a more detailed exploration of the interplay of literary communication and speech acts (and, specifically, the notion of felicitous speech acts), see J. L. Austin, *How to do Things with Words* (Cambridge: Harvard University Press, 1962); Mary Louise Pratt, *Toward a Speech Act Theory of Literary Discourse* (Bloomington: Indiana University Press, 1977); Shoshana Felman, *The Literary Speech Act* (Ithaca: Cornell University Press, 1983); Stanley Fish, *Is There a Text in This Class?* (Cambridge: Harvard University Press, 1980); John R. Searle, *Expression and Meaning: Studies in the Theory of Speech Acts* (Cambridge: Cambridge University Press, 1979).

assumes here as a central element in the play. Lope is showing us that language is what the play is about; ironically, he is doing so by means of scenes which display language's potential for both creative use and obfuscation.

We thus see that the early portraits of the two sisters display the women's disparity through the types of language that they employ. For completely antithetical reasons, neither sister is successful in the art of communication. Indeed, the girls' father summarizes the need for a middle ground between the two extremes: "pues la virtud es bien que el medio siga:/que Finea supiera más que sabe,/y Nise menos" (I. iii. 238-40).

At this stage in the play, Lope has already begun to subtly prepare us for the transformations that will take place. By means of the emphasis that he gives to words and their creative and transforming power, the dramatist has opened the door to the changes that will occur. Those changes result from the power of love; they will be reflected in the linguistic transformations of the two sisters, principally those of Finea. Robert ter Horst argues that, while the "central event [of the play] unmistakably is Finea's awakening to the mind of love," La dama boba offers, like Finea, multiple layers of disguises.[8] Our understanding of these levels necessarily involves Laurencio's role as both suitor and teacher to Finea. He transforms the "linda bestia" into a shrewd woman by teaching her the power of love: "que es la luz del entendimiento amor" (I. x. 830-31). The changes that Finea exhibits by the end of the play will be reflected in her linguistic virtuosity to the point that she ultimately uses language as a device to accomplish her marriage to the man she loves.

Finea's transformation is a slow process. She occasionally regresses; for example, she ingenuously tells her father that Laurencio has written her love letters and even embraced her. Otavio warns his daughter not to allow herself to be embraced again: "Sólo vuestro marido ha de ser digno/de esos brazos" (II. vii. 1527-8). This warning offers ironic possibilities for the future, because Finea as "boba" always functions on the literal level of linguistic meaning. Indeed, in a subsequent scene, Finea offers Laurencio a solution to her father's concern: she allows him to "disembrace" her by repeating the action in reverse. This example displays Finea's reasoning that since "abrazar" is negative, "desabrazar" must be positive; her reasoning is revealed first in terms of verbal invention, and then is translated into action. Her solution leads not to an undoing, but to a redoing, of the action that had gotten her into trouble.

This scene offers the reader/spectator two possible readings. The first might suggest that Finea is, indeed, a beginning student at

---

[8] ter Horst, pp. 347 and 349.

learning how language and linguistic control function: she cannot become an expert overnight. The dramatic action requires her to understand gradually, by means of trial and error; her occasional steps backward illustrate the evolutionary process of her transformation. A second reading however, would posit a more ironic view of the scene. Finea's "disembracing" technique suggests that she may have assimilated Laurencio's lessons at this relatively early point in the play. She thus establishes herself as a controlling character, using her earlier linguistic ingenuousness as a means of effecting a repetition of the embrace. Although apparently mutually exclusive, both readings are valid from a linguistic point of view. The scene is revealing because it explores how language functions to transform and control. It deals with the notion that the creative use of language, the invention of a verb like "desabrazar," can lead to ambiguous interpretations. Other characters' clarification of the words they use does not always create felicitous results. Nise proved this earlier in the sonnet scene; her sister proves it here. As noted earlier, in her article on *El castigo sin venganza*, McKendrick observed that Lope was aware that language can misinform, mislead, and conceal; we can now conclude that when language is used (as it is in *La dama boba*) as a tool for creating irony and humor, it can also reveal multiple levels of meaning to the reader / spectator.

No matter which interpretation of the scene described above is chosen, the *dama boba* is gradually changing, due to the lessons Laurencio has been giving her. Correspondingly, Nise begins to lose some of her earlier arrogance and confidence. When Nise notes the changes in her sister—"Yo te vi menos discreta"—Finea responds, "Y yo más segura a ti" (II. xii. 1672-3). Finea's new character reflects an increasing awareness of, and appropriate correspondence between, language and action. As she sees her father approach, she decides—for the first time—to hold her tongue: "Mi padre es éste; silencio / Callad lengua; ojos, hablad" (II. xv. 1786-7).

Finea is, however, still no match for Laurencio's manipulations and linguistic skill. When she suggests falling out of love with him in order to end her jealousies, Laurencio offers a solution involving the aid of his friends:

> Si dices delante destos
> cómo me das la palabra
> de ser mi esposa y mujer,
> todos los celos se acaban.
> (II. xviii. 1889-92)

Laurencio calls in his friends and servants to serve as witnesses to his new deception, and Finea promises to marry him. The key point here is, again, the use of language—in all of its multiple levels—to manipulate. Laurencio not only deceives with words, but uses a verbal promise to marry as a means of accomplishing his goals. He does not ask Finea to give him her hand; rather, Laurencio stresses the power of the word in a witnessed agreement.

This lesson in linguistic manipulation is a major aspect of Finea's education. In the month intervening between Acts II and III, she obviously assimilates much more. As Act III opens, Finea extols the virtues of her new-found love, for love has transformed her from *boba* to *discreta*. Yet, the theme of her soliloquy is not the only noticeable change. Finea's new sensibility is reflected in the type of language she employs, seen in her sophisticated use of metaphor, personification, and stylized Baroque oppositions. In this soliloquy, Finea addresses love in a style designed to display her new state of being:

> Tú desataste y rompiste
> la escuridad de mi ingenio;
> tú fuiste el divino genio
> que me enseñaste, y me diste
> la luz con que me pusiste
> el nuevo ser en que estoy.
> (III. i. 2053-8)

Finea has become so conscious of the power of language that she begins to show herself superior even to her teacher. She proposes a plan designed to get another suitor, Liseo, to leave her alone; in the process, *she* becomes the controlling character and teacher:

> El remedio es fácil.
> Si, porque mi rudo ingenio,
> que todos aborrecían,
> se ha transformado en discreto,
> Liseo me quiere bien,
> con volver a ser tan necio
> como primero le tuve,
> me aborrecerá Liseo.
> (III. ix. 2478-86)

Finea succeeds admirably in feigning her previous state and deceiving Liseo. She adopts her former half-witted speech patterns and asks him such bizarre questions that he assumes she is crazy. He vows to return to Nise, concluding that Finea "es loca sobre necia,/ que es la peor guarnición" (III. x. 2610-11).

Finea's deception has been a painful one. After Liseo leaves and Laurencio returns, she exclaims, "siento en extremo/volverme a boba, aun fingida./Y, pues fingida lo siento,/los que son bobos de veras,/

¿cómo viven?.../Háblame, Laurencio mío,/sutilmente, porque quiero/desquitarme de ser boba" (III. xi. 2616-20; 2627-9). Finea has again self-consciously stressed language as the focal point of her new existence. She has duped Liseo by manipulating words, and she returns to her new reality by appealing to Laurencio's ability to awaken her through language.

Yet, Finea's consciousness of her new state and corresponding ability to control language is paralleled by Nise's awareness that she is losing control. She seeks to reestablish her position of superiority in a telling scene with her father. Nise initiates the scene by stating, "Yo quiero hablar claro," self-consciously calling attention to language's power. Her words are ironic, because although Nise pointedly promises to speak clearly, she uses this opportunity to manipulate her father by means of half-truths. She suggests that Otavio prevent Laurencio from entering their house, because he has obstructed Finea's marriage to Liseo and created strife in the family. Yet, the discreet Nise only reveals part of the truth. What she does not say is that she, herself, is jealous of Laurencio and Finea's love.

Recognizing that she is no longer the controlling character, Nise has thus attempted to reestablish her position of superiority by using words to conceal and misinform. Her desperate attempts to restructure her world through the use of deceptive language, however, only further reveal her lack of control. She is trying to play a linguistic game at which she is inexperienced; she is further sabotaged by the emotions that are overpowering her intellectual control.

Nise's efforts to change the course of the dramatic action are temporarily successful, for Otavio attempts to remove Laurencio from his home. Laurencio, however, is able to counter this strategy by announcing that he has been married to Finea for a month, because she gave him her word. Otavio claims that Finea was too dull to make such a promise—and effect such a social contract—and asks her a revealing question:

OTAVIO	Di, Finea: ¿no eres simple?
FINEA	Cuando quiero.
OTAVIO	¿Y cuando no?
FINEA	No.

(III. xv. 2795-7)

Finea's words should prepare Otavio for her final deception, but he refuses to heed the implications of her message.

Finea resolves to hide Laurencio, sending him to the attic and telling her father that he has gone to Toledo. Otavio exclaims that Finea is too naive to be trusted around men; he advises her to stay away from them forever. This advice fits perfectly with Finea's plan, and she carefully leads her father into her trap by means of the conscious manipulation of words. Finea uses language to convey conflicting levels of meaning (literal and metaphoric) as she and her father discuss where she should hide from men. Finea suggests, "¿Será bien en un desván,/donde los gatos están?/¿Quieres tú que allí me meta?" (III. xviii. 2860-2). Otavio replies that any place she chooses is acceptable, as long as no one else sees her. Finea is thus able to triumphantly conlcude, "Pues, ¡alto! en el desván sea;/tú lo mandas, será justo./Yo advierte que lo has mandado" (III. xviii. 2865-7). Finea hurries off to obey her father's "order": "No yerra quien obedece./No me ha de ver hombre más,/sino quien mi esposo fuere" (III. xix. 2876-8). Finea has thus manipulated language to control the outcome of the dramatic action.

As the play draws to a close, a servant rushes in with the news that two men are in the attic with Finea and her maid. Otavio runs off to defend his honor and threatens to kill Laurencio. Finea again assumes the controlling role, as she explains her earlier "lie" that Laurencio was in Toledo:

> Padre,
> si aqueste desván se nombra
> "Toledo," verdad le dije.
> Alto está, pero no importa;
> que más lo estaba el Alcázar
> y la puente de Segovia
> y hubo Juanelos que a él
> subieron agua sin sogas.
> ¿El no me mandó esconder?
> Pues suya es la culpa toda.
> (III. xxvi. 3129-38)

Finea has succeeded in controlling language and in implementing her desires; the play ends with the promise of multiple weddings. It is, indeed, fitting that words and labels are used to effect her plan, for Finea has learned about the power of language as a by-product of the lessons of love she learned from Laurencio. As a result, she explains her enlightenment: "Por hablarte supe hablar ... amor me ha enseñado." By means of the utlimate linguistic deception of naming her garret "Toledo," Finea has illustrated the arbitrary nature of the link between signifier and signified; furthermore, she has shown how words can be used both in accordance with and against the linguistic conventions that govern our uses of language. Finea's manipulative use of words self-consciously underscores the power of language, calling attention to its fundamental importance in the play. Lope has shown us how language, used both creatively and destructively, illuminates the duality of illusion and reality that has been a constant motif throughout the drama.

Finea's early ambiguous speech patterns and later intentional obscurities are devices used to create a comic effect. This creative use of words is, in many ways, similar to the type of witty exchanges found in other Golden Age comedies. What makes *La dama boba* different is a focus on the communicative act itself. Lope constantly calls our attention to the power of words; he pairs Nise's literary academies and analyses of esthetic language with Finea's ongoing lessons in how language functions and transforms, as she, herself, changes. We have seen both principal and secondary characters use language self-consciously; Lope seems to be developing a subtle substructure based on language, on naming, on manipulation. When the women's suitors duel, they do so with words, and not with swords. Direct references to language resurface continually throughout the play. As certain characters seek to influence the actions of others, they express their desire in terms of language; "¡Nunca, plega a Dios, hablaras!" or "¡Cortaréle aquella lengua!" are typical expletives. *La dama boba* is about control and manipulation, but it is primarily about how language effects that control. Lope inplicitly encourages us to participate in the process of discovering how words function in the play, leading us to a kind of linguistic awareness which, not surprisingly, parallels the awakening of Finea to language's potential.

INDIANA UNIVERSITY

The Performative Status
of Verbal Offenses in
A secreto agravio, secreta venganza

MYRA GANN

F THE THREE FAMOUS "dramas de honor" by Calde-
rón, the one which has received the most atten-
tion critically has been *El médico de su honra*,
possibly because it is the most ambiguous and
perplexing of the three. It has been asserted,
however, that *A secreto agravio, secreta venganza* is
the one in which Calderón deals with the
subject matter most definitively;[1] and it is to
this play that I wish to turn in attempting to analyze once more the
enigmatic and arbitrary functioning of the honor code. In it we see
how in two separate cases highly honorable men whose lives have
been dedicated to living by the rules of honor have no defense against
words which unjustly accuse and defame them. Calderón is clearly
stating that the root of the "problem" of the honor code—that is, why
it is so difficult to follow, why it is unjust and unyeilding, why it leads
men to feel that they have no choice but to murder their wives—is
that it allows one man to destroy another by means of a verbal
formula which is not subject to any true-false verification. He is also
pointing to silence—so frequently a poetic motif in these plays—as
the only way to live entirely within the confines of the code. But, as
he shows us in this play, such silence is impossible to maintain, since
it would require that the lover dispense with the *queja*, that a man
suppress all expressions of *celos*, even to himself, that intimate friends

---

[1] Edwin Honig, "Calderón's Secret Vengeance: Dehumanizing Honor,"
in David A. Kossoff and José Amor y Vázquez, eds., *Studies in Honor of
William L. Fichter*, Castalia, Madrid, 1971, p. 205.

communicate only indirectly on the most important subject of a nobleman's existence.[2]

It is no coincidence that the secondary plot of this play is introduced after only 47 verses have been pronounced. Don Lope, in those first lines, has requested from the king permission to "colgar las armas" and devote himself to married life, into which he is about to enter (Leonor is journeying to meet him now). Having received the approval of the King, Lope is expressing his joy when his friend Juan arrives with a story which puts a damper on his happiness. Juan and Lope are old army buddies, having fought the wars in "la India" together until Lope was called home because of the death of his father. Juan stayed on and continued to earn "fama de amigos y de opinión." He fell in love with a beautiful, discreet woman, who returned his love even though she had another suitor "de mucha resolución, muy valiente, muy cortés, bizarro y cuerdo" (meaning, of course, that Juan was even more than all of that). One day Violante ventured out to the port to watch the arrival of a ship, and in the crowd were Juan and also his rival, Manuel. Don Juan recounts the three-way exchange which ensued:

> Dijo un capitán, "¡Qué bella
> mujer!" A quien respondió
> don Manuel: "Y como tal
> ha sido la condición."
> "Será cruel." "No por eso
> lo digo—le replicó—,
> sino por ver que ha escogido,
> como hermosa, lo peor."
> Yo entonces dije: "Ninguno
> sus favores mereció,
> porque no hay quien los merezca;
> y si hay alguno, soy yo."
> "Mentís," dijo.
>   (I, vv. 185-197)[3]

That was all it took, says Juan, for years of accumulating honor to "go down the drain," even though the accusation was obviously a "sinrazón":

---

[2] Peter Dunn, in his well-known article "Honor and the Christian Background in Calderón," *BHS*, 37 (1960), 75-105, argues convincingly that in these plays honor has in fact reached the status of a religion and for this reason had to be the target of criticism for religious writers such as Calderón.

[3] All quotes are taken from Valbuena Briones' edition of the play in Clásicos Castellanos, Madrid, 1956.

¡Oh tirano error
de los hombres!   ¡Oh vil ley
del mundo!   ¡Que una razón,
o que una sinrazón pueda
manchar el altivo honor
tantos años adquirido,
y que la antigua opinión
de honrado quede postrada
a lo fácil de una voz!
(I, vv. 204-212)

Manuel's "mentís" has dishonored Juan, as he well knows, and he shows this by reacting as convention would have it:

Apenas él pronunció
tales razones, don Lope,
cuando mi espada veloz
pasó de la vaina al pecho.
(I, vv. 222-225)

Juan's response would be called, in terms of modern speech-act theory, "uptake," meaning that he has understood the (dishonoring) intention of the speaker of the words and is responding in a conventional way indicating that the intention has been thus interpreted. Actually, several insights discovered by speech-act theorists are relevant to analyzing the vulnerability of the subscribers to the honor code as seen in the *comedia*. It is pertinent, I feel, to observe that "mentís" functions exactly as the performative utterance which led J. L. Austin to study speech as action.

One of Austin's first observations was that

Utterances can be found... such that...
a. they do not 'describe' or 'report' or constate any-thing at all, are not 'true' or 'false'; and
b. the uttering of the sentence is, or is a part of, the doing of an action, which again would not *normally* be described as saying something.
(Austin, *How to Do...*, p. 5)

These utterances he called "performatives," since in them *doing* and *saying* are one and the same: upon saying "I promise," "I swear," or "I now pronounce you man and wife" one respectively promises, swears or pronounces a couple man and wife (provided the "appropriate conditions" are satisfied, i.e., that the speaker has the authority to carry out such acts, that the hearer believes the speaker to be sincere, etc.). Austin's most significant observation about this type of utterance was that because of its unique nature—because proposition (what is said) and illocutionary force (what is done) coincide—they are not subject to any test of truth or falsity, but rather should be judged as sincere or insincere, successful or unsuccessful, felicitous or infelicitous, etc. (depending on their satisfying the appropriate conditions). An understanding of this type of "speech act" helps us to fathom the power of the actual spoken (uttered) word and better appreciate the dilemma of the protagonists of Calderón's "dramas de honor": Don Gutierre, Don Lope de Figueroa, and Don Juan de Roca all find themselves faced with the danger of having a dishonor *voiced* and therefore constituted, regardless of the guilt or innocence of their wives. In order to preempt the uttering of the doubt which would constitute the dishonor, they all choose to wipe out the subject matter itself and thus silence the voice of the common tongue in a final way.

As I indicated earlier, all of this is most clearly understood in *A secreto agravio, secreta venganza* because in it we have, besides the implied "your wife is dishonoring you," which is common to all three plays, the clear example of the man who has had to deal with the most explicit, offensive, "performative" insult: the "mentís." "Mentís" itself does not, of course, fall strictly into Austin's category of "explicit performatives" since it is the second person, and not the first person, of an active indicative verb. However, as the action of this play shows, it is an utterance (cf. the above-quoted Austin passage) a) the truth or falsity of which is totally irrelevant (once uttered it cannot be retracted and will never by forgotten); and b) the uttering of which *is* the dishonoring of the hearer, an action which "would not *normally* be described as saying something": it would be novel for us to think of "dishonoring" as "saying something" rather than "doing something." It is then, at least, a primary performative.[4] "Mentís" is also the perfect paradigm of the verbal act of dishonoring because, since it can only be expressed directly, face-to-face, in the context of some immediately previous discourse, there is no way the hearer can pretend not to have heard it and therefore no way he can protect his honor from it. The other type of verbal offense, the implication that one's wife is being unfaithful, can be either direct (in which case it has the same force as the performative "mentís") or indirect, as when it is simply spread abroad by gossip ("la murmuración del vulgo"). From Juan's story the protagonist in *A secreto agravio* learns that the indirect type is preferable and can still be dealt with within the confines of the honor code. But, as we see him at the end of the play preparing to fight a war from which we know no one returned, we realize that he has fared no better than Juan.

---

4 These function as explicit performatives and can be rephrased as such (in our case, perhaps, "Yo declaro que mientes"), but have been conventionalized in other forms.

Speech-act theory is mainly concerned with formulating the appropriateness conditions of the different speech acts as used by particular linguistic communities. We have already mentioned or implied some of these conditions for the successful execution of "mentís." Hypothetically, and subject to testing by examination of other plays, let us say that: 1) The speaker and hearer must both be male, since honor actually only "belongs" to men: a woman can lose her honor, which in her case is synonymous with "virtue"⁵ or cause a man to lose his, but cannot gain it since she cannot engage in war or other honor-producing activities. 2) The speaker and hearer must both *have* honor, at least the inherited kind, since otherwise they could not lose it.⁶ This means that characters lacking noble blood are ineligible (thus "mentís" in the mouth of a *gracioso* is not our performative "mentís"). 3) There must be a verbal context in which some immediate discourse provokes the "mentís" and the reference for this discourse must be absent or unverifiable as true or false. In *A secreto agravio*, the three-way exchange provides the context for the insult. Juan cannot immediately prove that no man has yet merited the favors and can only show that were any man to merit them, it would be he, by drawing his sword, defending his name by showing valor. 4) It should also be noted that transgressions of the honor code which occur in farcical plays such as *La discreta enamorada* or *La dama boba* (both imply premarital bedroom scenes) do not have the "illocutionary force" or "perlocutionary effects" of our "mentís." All is forgotten in this genre of plays if there is a marriage at the end to legitimize and cover up. Thus, it will probably be true that only in "serious" plays will a "mentís" function in the highly performative way we are studying here.⁷

From another, more general perspective, it is obvious that both the form and the content of the *comedia* are highly conventional and ritualistic in nature. Conventions such as "rondar la calle," "mandar un papel," "dar una prenda," and "hablar desde el balcón" are easily recognized as standard procedures to be followed during the courting

---

⁵ Cf. Gustavo Correa's treatment of the difference in honor for men and women in "El doble aspecto de la honra en el teatro del siglo XVII," *HR*, 26 (1958), 99-107.

⁶ That honor is a commodity which can be acquired and lost in different quantities is also seen clearly in this play. In his first speech Juan comments upon the motives which led Lope and him to enlist in the Indian campaign: "No codicia de riqueza,/sino condicia de honor/obligó nuestros deseos/a tan atrevida acción." (I, vv. 91-94).

⁷ Bruce W. Wardropper, in his article "El problema de la responsabilidad en la comedia de capa y espada de Calderón" (*Actas del Segundo Congreso Internacional de Hispanistas*, Nimega, 1967, pp. 689-94), discusses at length the fact that the consequences for breaking the honor code are different in the farcical plays.

ritual. The *gracioso* is fond of making reference both to these "internal" conventions of the *comedia* and to such "external" ones as the use of certain meters to express certain passions, the custom of having male and female servants echo the love affair of the protagonists "en tono menor," etc. In this context, then, it is not difficult to grant "conventional" status to the uttering of "mentís." We can say that when one man of honor says it to another in a "serious" play, within the context of some unverifiable discourse, the second man is permanently dishonored. But to understand the "permanently" of this formula we must follow to the end Don Juan's trajectory during *A secreto agravio*; it is perhaps the indelible permanence of verbal dishonor in this play that singles it out as Calderón's "definitive honor play."

As a result of killing the man who dishonored him (as the code required that he do), Juan had to go into hiding. He ultimately escaped from Goa and returned to Portugal with his life, but with little more: he lost the woman he loved and was defending, as well as the social status and the riches he enjoyed in Goa:

> ¡Injusto engaño
> de la vida!   O su pasión
> no dé por infame al hombre
> que sufre su deshonor,
> o le dé por disculpado
> si se venga; que es error
> dar a la afrenta castigo,
> y no al castigo perdón.
> (I, vv. 255-262)

After hearing Juan's story, Lope invites him to live with him and share his own reputation and "hacienda." Juan accepts and, due to his experience in matters of honor, functions from here on as an expert watchdog. When in the second act Lope is moved to take up arms again and aid the king in his new African campaign, Juan advises against his leaving Leonor alone and, unsure if Lope has understood the implications of his words, he feigns (in the next act) asking advice of Lope in order to actually give him advice. He is forced to take recourse to this variant of "engañar con la verdad" because he understands all too well that the verbalization of a doubt about honor constitutes dishonor and can lead to disaster. He states this clearly in the last two lines of the following portion of his soliloquy:

> ¿Podré yo ver murmurar
> que este castellano adore
> a Leonor, que la enamore,
> y le dé lugar Leonor,
> y padeciendo su honor,

yo lo sepa y él quedara
satisfecho, siendo mía
la venganza, en este día
al castellano matara.
A él sin él yo le vengara,
prudente, advertido y sabio;
mas de la intención del labio
satisfacción no se alcanza,
si el brazo de la venganza
no es del cuerpo del agravio.
Yo a don Lope le diré
clara y descubiertamente
que no hable al rey ni se ausente.
Mas si me dice por qué,
¿cómo le responderé
la causa? Duda mayor
es ésta; que al que el valor
eterno honor le previene,
quien dice que no le tiene
es quien le quita el honor.
      (Underlining is in Valbuena Briones' text)
      (III, vv. 21-47)

We know that Don Lope also subscribes to this formula and that
Juan's caution is therefore warranted: we saw it in Lope's response to
Juan's first bit of advice. In the soliloquy which followed his conversation with Juan (we jump back now to the second act), he carried this
same idea to the extreme and commented at length on the irreparable
damage done by a verbalized hint of dishonor, even when the speaker
has no apparent hearer (he feels that he has divided himself into two
parts, the second one being the hearer, and thus the dishonor is
constituted). He began that soliloquy by expressing his general state
of frustration and dissatisfaction; then, after deciding that he could no
longer repress all that was bothering him ("Ahora bien: fuerza es
quejarme"), he tried to proceed cautiously, but nonetheless fell into
the trap of giving voice to his own offense:

¿Osará decir la lengua
qué tengo?... Lengua, detente,
no pronuncies, no articules
mi afrenta; que si me ofendes,
podrá ser que castigada,
con mi vida o con mi muerte,
siendo ofensor y ofendido,
yo me agravie y yo me vengue.

No digas que tengo celos...
Ya lo dije, ya no puede
volverse al pecho la voz.
¿Posible es que tal dijese
sin que, desde el corazón
al labio, consuma y queme
el pecho este aliento, esta
respiración fácil, este
veneno infame, de todos
tan distinto y diferente,
que otros desde el labio al pecho
hacer sus efectos suelen,
y este desde el pecho al labio?
¿A qué aspid, a qué serpiente
mató su propio veneno?
                    (II, vv. 233-255)

Others (literally) kill themselves by drinking poison—passing it from
lips to breast. Lope, upon expressing the venomous thoughts which
are buried in his breast by breaking the silence the honor code would
impose, poisons himself in a reverse (metaphorical) fashion.

Returning to Juan's masked advice, then, we see how implied
meaning is successfully communicated between two people who abide
by the same verbal and social conventions and are bound by the same
vow of silence on matters of honor. Don Juan posits the case of a man
who chances to hear one hidalgo "desmentir" another. The second
one, his friend, did not hear the insult. Juan wonders, then,

¿si éste tendrá obligación
de decirlo claramente
al otro, que está inocente;
o si dejar es razón
que padezca su opinión,
pues él no basta a vengalle?
Si lo calla es agravialle,
y si lo dice es error
de amigo.
                    (III, vv. 91-99)

Lope decides, of course, that silence is the most honorable solution,
since "no puede un hombre estar/ignorante y agraviado" (vv. 113-
114). Furthermore, he says, if he were to find himself in the situation
of the person who was "desmentido" and found out about the offense
from a friend, he would *first* avenge himself upon his *friend* for having
voiced the offense someone else committed:

Y yo de mí sé decir
que si un amigo cual vos
(siendo quien somos los dos)
tal me llegara a decir,
tal pudiera presumir
de mí, tal imaginara,
que el primero en quien vengara
mi desdicha, fuera en él;
porque es cosa muy cruel
para dicha cara a cara.
Y no sé que en tal rigor
haya razón que no asombre,
con que se le pueda a un hombre
decir: "No tenéis honor."
(III, vv. 121-134)

The utterer, in reporting an offense committed by a third, absent party, is himself offending, but in a more serious way, since he performs face-to-face the all-powerful speech act of dishonoring: his offense is even greater than that of the original offender! To prove his point, Lope again takes his argument to an absurd extreme, imagining himself again as both speaker and hearer and asserting as he did in his soliloquy that were he himself the utterer-offender, he would avenge the offense with death:

Testigo
es Dios (otra vez lo digo),
que si yo me lo dijera,
a mí la muerte me diera,
y soy mi mayor amigo.
(III, vv. 136-140)

But even though silence and secretiveness have been declared necessary for the maintaining of one's honor, Lope has still not fully understood the seriousness and permanence of being even once the object of a performative act of dishonoring. For after this scene with don Juan, he talks with himself again, first complaining bitterly about the injustice of a code which offers no protection to a man who has always obeyed all the rules (vv. 229-255), then resigning himself to accepting the code with all its defects ("Yo vivo para vengarlas [las costumbres necias],/no para enmendarlas vivo." vv. 286-287), and finally proclaiming that he will cleanse his stained reputation with "la más pública venganza... que el mundo hay visto" (vv. 291-292). He changes his plan, though, when Don Juan makes his final contribution to the plot of the play by appearing in a later scene (some time

has apparently passed) to recount the following "last straw" in his
loss-of-honor story:

> ¡Ay, don Lope, muerto estoy!
> Hoy nuevamente recibo
> la afrenta, que en la venganza
> pensé que estaba en su olvido
> más, ay de mí, ha sido engaño.
> Porque bastante no ha sido
> la venganza a sepultar
> un agravio recibido.
> Cuando me aparté de vos,
> llegué hasta este propio sitio
> que bate el mar, con el fin
> que vos propio habéis venido,
> que es de volver a la quinta
> adonde habéis reducido
> vuestra casa, previniendo
> vuestra ausencia. [Divertido]
> llegué, pues, y en esta parte
> estaban en un corrillo
> unos hombres, y al pasar
> el uno a los otros dijo:
> "Aquéste es don Juan de Silva."
> Yo, oyendo mi nombre mismo,
> que es lo que se oye más fácil,
> apliqué entrambos oídos.
> Otro preguntó: "Y quién es
> este don Juan?" "No has oído
> (le respondió) su suceso?
> Pues éste fue desmentido
> de Manuel de Sosa." Yo,
> que ya no pude sufrirlo,
> saco la espada, y a un tiempo
> tales razones le digo:
> "Yo soy aquel que maté
> a don Manuel, mi enemigo,
> tan presto, que de mi agravio
> la última razón no dijo.
> Yo soy el *desagraviado*,
> Que no soy el *desmentido*."
>
>   (Underlining is in Valbuena Briones' text)
>   (III, vv. 307-344)

Juan was willing to break the legal code which governed him (according to which murder was forbidden even for motives of honor) in order to uphold the social one he lives by; but the latter is always subject to the arbitrariness of the word, which, in turn, may be used quite irresponsibly. The honor code, as tacitly agreed upon by those who adhere to it (we recall that Lope, even as he questioned the "necias costumbres" it embodies, decided to uphold it), permits *agravios* to be easily constituted and never erased. A "mentís" will accompany a man until he dies.

And now, since care has been taken throughout the play to avoid openly suggesting to Lope that his wife may be dishonoring him (no adultery is ever actually committed, by the way, and the critics are divided as to Leonor's intention—my own reading finds her innocent), Lope can prevent what has happened to Juan from happening to himself by resorting to a secret vengeance rather than carrying out a public one as he was first inclined to do. Juan has taught Lope that only a "secreta venganza" is appropriate when the offense has not yet reached performative status. Leonor is innocent; Lope cannot be blamed for taking the only viable course of action open to him. Clearly the system is at fault: Calderón is exposing the injustice of a code which permits one man to dishonor another by employing a formula which is exempt from the test of "true" or "false" and the pronouncing of which can never be revoked.

STATE UNIVERSITY OF NEW YORK, POTSDAM

"That Dangerous Supplement": *La Verdad Sospechosa* and the Literary Speech Situation

Harold A. Veeser

Y TITLE APPLIES in several ways to this paper and the circumstances that produced it. First, the title should remind us that the central figure in Alarcón's play enters the dramatic setting as a returning exile and remains, as did his creator, partly unassimilated to the tightly-knit culture of Madrid. A second potentially disruptive supplement consists in the long narrative inserts with which that central figure interrupts the dramatic action. Stretching on occasion to more than one hundred lines, these little novellas seem inimical to the rapid development that we associate with the Spanish *comedia*, and for that matter with drama in general. Since these passages represent a continuing problem for critics, I shall attempt, in the four parts of my paper, to explain first the causes and then the personal, social, and literary consequences of these extended narrative texts. "Display texts," as M.L. Pratt defines them, less often transmit information than provide their narrator with opportunities to elaborate a tale and display his narrative gift.[1] The term seems just right for what the hero does with his words. In terms of my four-part structure, the

---

    [1] Mary Louise Pratt, *Toward a Speech Act Theory of Literary Discourse* (Bloomington: Indiana University Press, 1977), 136-48. A display text is "tellable (in the Labovian sense). It contrasts sharply with the kind of relevance we expect of assertions made in answer to or in anticipation of a question, these being paradigm examples of what Grice means by a 'maximally effective exchange of information.'" Thus, "in making an assertion whose relevance is tellability, a speaker is not only reporting but also verbally *displaying* a state of affairs, inviting his addressee(s) to join him in contemplating it, evaluating it, and responding to it."

hero's broken history leads him to reconstruct his identity by means of made-up histories. These bring an awareness of time to his static milieu and drive an otherwise standard *comedia* toward parody and farce.

The other notions of supplementarity that bear on this paper come from speech-act theory. No aspect of that theory has excited more vigorous complaints than its supposition that words uttered on stage or written in a poem do not *do things* in just the same way that words uttered under "normal circumstances" do things. J. L. Austin believes, for example, that a promise spoken in a play merely battens "parasitically" on real promises.[2] That idea has drawn challenges from such literary powerbrokers as Stanley Fish and Jacques Derrida. It abets our lingering superstition, according to Derrida, that writing is somehow secondary to an actual speaking presence. Against Austin's notion of hollow, void, and parasitical literary utterance, Derrida inverts the hierarchy. Were it impossible for a fictional character to make a promise, he argues, then no one in real life could either. He stresses that it is the iterability or citability, perhaps the unoriginality, of standard formulae that makes any promise (or other act in language) possible.[3] Umberto Eco puts the same thesis another way. "If something cannot be used to tell a lie," he writes in *A Theory of Semiotics*, "conversely it cannot be used to tell the truth."[4] More obviously repeatable and reproducible than spoken sound, writing is "dangerous" simply because it reminds us that every utterance is, if not actually fiction, then wholly conventional and as much dependent on existing verbal formulae as is any acknowledged fiction. Don García embodies such dangers when, returning from exile, he imitates literary models in order to overcome his estrangement and invent an identity. His strategy demystifies the other characters'

---

[2] J. L. Austin, *How To Do Things With Words* (Cambridge, Mass.: Harvard University Press, 1962; reprinted 1975), 22. "A performative utterance will, for example, be in a peculiar way hollow or void if said by an actor on the stage or introduced in a poem, or spoken in a soliloquy.... Language in such circumstances is in special ways—intelligibly—used not seriously, but in ways parasitic upon its normal use—ways which fall under the doctrine of the *etiolations* of language. All this we are excluding from consideration."

[3] Jaques Derrida, *Marges de la philosophie* (Paris: Minuit, 1972), trans. as *Margins of Philosophy* (Chicago: University of Chicago Press); and "Signature Event Context," *Glyph 1* (1977), 172-97. See also John Searle's reply to Derrida, "Reiterating the Differences," *Glyph 1* (1977). For an overview of the debate between deconstruction and speech-act theory, see Jonathan Culler, *On Deconstruction* (Ithaca: Cornell University press, 1982), 110-34, and Christopher Norris, *Deconstruction: Theory and Practice* (London and New York: Methuen, New Accent Series, 1982), 108-16 and *The Deconstructive Turn* (London: Methuen, 1983), 13-33.

[4] Umberto Eco, *A Theory of Semiotics* (Bloomington: Indiana University Press, 1976).

belief in the fixity and timelessness of their world. His excesses—his supplementarity—in that way render the truth suspicious: *La Verdad Sospechosa*. But others before me had found Alarcón's a "speech-act play."

Critical debate has often turned on the questionable nature of that activity in *La Verdad Sospechosa*, particularly on the morality of the character who authors the long "display texts." Many have felt that this narrator deserves, for telling tales, the punishment he receives (he does not in the end get the girl, at least not the girl he wants). But to focus on this punitive measure is to overlook much that counteracts it. Within the calculus of Roman New Comedy, in which society moves from sterility to fecundity, this play has a satisfying resolution.[5] Such an ending in the *comedia* is, of course, inevitable. But significantly Don García's three major lies provide the efficient cause of this ultimate effect. Before García intervenes, Juan seems condemned to bachelorhood, and Lucrecia and Jacinta, to lead apes in hell. Then García shakes up Juan and proposes to Lucrecia; with the double marriage that concludes the play, integrating all the eligible youths with society and preparing them to reproduce it, we would seem to have reached an entirely happy ending.

Why then, with all the generic signposts to the contrary, have readers found the ending manifestly *un*happy? This antinomy between comic structure and tragic flavor has disturbed Alarcón's critics. Often such critics have resolved the apparent contradiction by ignoring the structure and scrutinizing García's faults and ultimate failure.

Voltaire, who called *La Verdad Sospechosa* "the first comedy of character," may have been the first critic to isolate a single personality as the principal object of interest.[6] A.A. Parker, with his classic essay on poetic justice in the *comedia*, adopts much the same emphasis. "The principle of poetic justice can deprive a Spanish comedy of a happy ending," Parker explains. Thus he disposes of the antinomy between comic structure and tragic impact. The *comedia* exists, in this view, at least partly in order to put certain characters to the ethical test.[7]

---

[5] Alarcón evidently based the play in part upon Terence's *Andria*, a classic example of New Comedy. See E. Perez, "Influencia de Plauto en el teatro de Ruiz de Alarcón," *Hispania*, 11 (1928), 131-49.

[6] Voltaire, Letter to the French Academy, 1776, in *Oeuvres completes*, ed. Louis Moland (Paris, 1877-1885), XXX, 364; my translation.

[7] A. A. Parker, "The Approach," reprinted as "The Spanish Drama of the Golden Age: A Method of Analysis and Interpretation" in *The Great Playwrights*, ed. Eric Bentley (New York, 1970), 686. Poetic justice consists in "the satisfaction or appropriateness felt when a deserving man should meet with good fortune or an undeserving man with ill fortune, whether or not the particular recompense is directly connected with his deserts . . . The 'punishment' of the character who has erred . . . need not be punishment brought about by any outside agent; it may only be a failure or frustration."

Subsequent debate has more narrowly put Don García on trial. The fact that "the unfortunate protagonist loses the woman he loves and is compelled to marry one he does not love," Parker rules, "is of course the frustration he deserves."Ángel Valbuena Prat appeals the decision: "el mentiroso don García atrae nuestras simpatías y sus enredos ofrecen un nivel poético que no merece castigo." Arguing for the prosecution, G. Ribbans charges that "the harsh ending is consonant with the errors Don García has made." E.C. Riley enters a plea of insanity, citing contemporary psychologists who regarded lying as a vice akin to drunkenness. J. Frutos Gómez, however, convicts García on an older statute—"La máxima 'secundum rationem vivere' es colaborada por todos las grandes figuras del teatro de Alarcón." Ellen Claydon indicts our hero on another count, for "it is important to emphasize the framework of the fault so as not to interpret it only in the light of social virtue, but rather as *Christian virtue*." Ebersole suggests extenuating circumstances: "su mala suerte ordena que... luche, y miente para evitar tener que cumplir los deseos de su padre." Against that idea DiLillo fulminates, "Not only has García duped and exploited his own father, but he takes satisfaction in having done so." Demanding the fullest penalty, DiLillo insists that "even the most lenient moral judge must recognize the unethical behavior in the deliberateness and pleasure," etc., etc.[8]

Although a discussion based on speech-act theory may never reach this level of pettifogging, the very nature of that theory places Don García in the dock once again. Although he now has to answer different charges (not that he acted immorally, but that he spoke infelicitously), the investigation continues to treat his dramatic char-

---

[8] Parker, 690. Angel Valbuena Prat, *El teatro español en su Siglo de Oro* (Barcelona: Editorial Planeta, 1969), 227-42; Geoffrey Ribbans, "Lying in the structure of *La Verdad Sospechosa*," in *Studies in Spanish Literture of the Golden Age presented to Edward M. Wilson*, ed. R. O. Jones (London: Tamesis Books, 1973); E. C. Riley, "Alarcón's Mentiroso in the light of contemporary theory of character," *Hispanic Studies in Honor of I. González Llubera*, ed. F. Pierce (Oxford: Oxford University Press, 1959), 287-97, cites Bacon, Huarte de San Juan, and other writers on character in order to show that the play turns on the opposition, in Don García, between *inclinación* (or nature) and *costumbre* (or environment); J. Frutos Gómez de las Cortinas, "La génesis de *Las Paredes oyen*," *RFE* 35 (1951), 92-105; Ellen Claydon, *Juan Ruiz de Alarcón: Baroque Dramatist* (Estudios de Hispanofila, 1970); A. V. Ebersole, *Juan Ruiz de Alarcón y Mendoza, Primera y segunda partes de las obras completas* (Madrid: Castalia, 1966), xiii; Leonard M. DiLillo, "Moral Purpose in Ruiz de Alarcón's *La Verdad Sospechosa, Hispania* 56 (1973), 257; see also John Brooks "La Verdad Sospechosa: The Source and Purpose," *Hispania* 15 (1932), 243-52, emphasizing didactic method "concerned with education," and Antonio Castro Leal, *Juan Ruiz de Alarcón: Su vida y su obra* (Mexico: Ediciones Cuadernos Americanos, 1943), 136, rejecting the moralistic reading: "La comedia no tiene ningún propósito didáctico."

acter as an established entity that bears full responsibility for its actions. Yet it is just this presumption that individuals act freely and compose their own sovereign destinies that this play compels us to reconsider.

When Don Beltrán muses, upon his son's return from Salamanca, "¡Qué hombre vienes!", he sets before us in the tenth line the problem that the next three acts are required to solve. This simple question opens all four of the principal topics. One is the return from a sort of exile: the speech informs us that García has just arrived from someplace else and appears (as he himself will say) to be a "forastero," a stranger even to his father. Another is identity: "what (kind of) man?" A third is history: García evidently has changed, and change takes place in time. Finally, language: Beltrán chooses to express his surprise in words rather than with gestures or (as an Apache might) with silence.[9]

Estrangement, identity, history, and language intersect, not only in Beltrán's interjection, but also throughout the play. These focal issues give the play a certain urgency for modern critics, plagued as we are by specters of uprooted, expatriate modernism. García's habit of creating his own fictional worlds to offset the anxiety of placelessness has been the canonical practice of modern exiles from Conrad to Beckett. His fictions, like theirs, force on those who know only one home the awareness that worlds exist beyond their own.

First we might ask whether Don García really does represent strangeness and displacement. Edward W. Said has been the foremost critic of this modern disorder. "The exile," he says,

> insists on his right to refuse to belong... Willfulness, exaggeration, overstatement: these are characteristic styles of being an exile, methods for compelling the world to accept your vision.

Although most people are chiefly aware of one culture and one place, the exile knows two. "This plurality of vision," Said remarks, "is contrapuntal." Every word activity or habit in the new environment occurs against the memory of such things in the old one. Knowing that the borders and barriers that enclose us within the safety of familiar territory can also become prisons, "exiles cross borders, break barriers of thought and experience." The exile, concludes Said, compensates for disorienting loss by creating new worlds to rule.[10]

---

[9] The Apache greet with silence even the closest family members after an extended absence of the sort don García has had. See K. H. Basso, "'To Give up on Words': Silence in Western Apache Culture," in *Language and Social Context*, ed. P. P. Giglioli (Harmondsworth: Penguin, 1972), 67-86.

[10] Edward W. Said, "The Mind of Winter," *Harper's* vol 269, No. 1612 (24 September 1984), 54-55. Professor Said's career has been distinguished by his matchless investigations of the literary and political importance of exile.

Though such worlds are often pure fictions, they bring unique pleasure and the awareness of simultaneous dimensions. The exile's portrait matches García's line for line. He first walks onstage dressed "de estudiante, de camino", the traveller's garb accentuating his strangeness. We soon hear his father explain how he has put Garcia on "el camino que seguía de las letras" (70-71) and later warn his son that he has returned to "otro mundo," the world of the Court. García for his part demands the right to remain different. It is because he refuses to do "lo que todos hazen" (859) that he spins tall tales. Extravagant, hyperbolic, outrageous—Said's styles of being an exile are also García's. He stands outside all doors, whether of women or professions (see, for example, 77, 824, 1340, and 1655); others perceive him to be breaking barriers and traversing permissible limits. He has real or feigned memories of Salamanca, the Sotillo, Peru, and the Indies and, most of all, feels confined in Madrid.

García's foreignness reaches beyond plot and theme to the dramatic type he represents. Although he does indeed aspire to the sort of wordly wittiness that we usually look for in the comedy of manners, and though he possesses the wealth and position of a Dorimant or an Alceste, nonetheless he remains a "bisoño" or beginner who needs a preceptor to teach him urbane habits. "¿Úsase en la corte?", he has to ask Tristán, as he investigates strategies for introducing himself to the beauty, Jacinta. If his coolness and verbal agility anticipate the English or French comic hero's, his lack of prudence and sound motives suggest the opposite theatrical type, the Pastor-Bobo whose near-idiocy delighted Juan de Encina's sixteenth-century audience.[11] If he outrages common mores, like Tirso's *burla-*

His own work has dialectically integrated two worlds of the exile, one comprised by expatriate literary modernists, the other by "uncountable masses of refugees." His *Orientalism* (New York: Pantheon, 1978), *The Question of Palestine* (London: Routledge and Kegan Paul, 1979), and *Covering Islam* (New York: Pantheon, 1981) explore with relentless thoroughness how apparently innocent activity in literature, or more recently in electronic media, directly affect immense numbers of people, helping to take their homelands or lives. His *Beginnings: Intention and Method* (New York: Basic Books, 1975) and *The World, the Text, and the Critic* (Cambridge: Harvard University Press, 1979) proceed from the fundamental insight that the modern critic who "cannot have direct recourse to tradition in solving the problems of writers like Joyce ... is aptly characterized in Lukacs' epithet for the novel as being transcendentally homeless" (*Beginnings,* 11). Even Said's first book, *Jospeh Conrad and the Fiction of Autobiography* (Cambridge: Harvard, 1966), is an extended confrontation, by way of the emigré Conrad and his writings, with the ache of exile. For a concise introduction to this important activist-critic, see Bruce Robbins, "Homelessness and Worldliness," *Diacritics* (Fall 1983), 69-77.

11 See John Brotherton, *The Pastor-Bobo in the Spanish Theatre Before the Time of Lope de Vega* (London: Tamesis Books Ltd., 1975).

dor, he also shifts unaccountably to the high heroic strain, insisting that the duel go forward, even invoking the "soy quien soy" formula that occurs so frequently in Golden Age plays about honor. Although his mendacious boast that he has split Don Juan's skull and his technical jargon for describing the duel place him with other *milites gloriosi*, nonetheless he *has* (as no typical braggart soldier would) fought valiantly. Don Juan, for one, cannot reconcile these contradictory traits: "Lo que me tiene dudoso / es que sea mentiroso / un hombre que es tan valiente" (1905-7). García's father expresses that same sense of bafflement when he explodes, "¿No te avergüenza que hayas / menester tu criado / acredite que hablas?" It appears to Beltrán that master and servant have changed places, and García has in fact taken up the *gracioso's* traditional function of arranging trysts.[12] Master and servant, hero and mock-hero, witty sophisticate and rustic *bobo* all, in Don García, infiltrate each other.

Sui generis, García seems all the more a stranger in his *comedia*, a dramatic form that generally features recognizable types. That unfamiliarity proves to be contagious, causing the virtuous heroine to waver in her commitment to Juan, the honorable Beltrán to forswear himself, the caballero Juan to stammer like a fool, and the canny *gracioso* Tristán to fall for a hoax. The hero's decentered quality might even be said to transform the comedic structure itself. His display texts, those hundred-line fibs, run counter to the imperatives of time and action that impel all drama. Thus by means of García's local speech action a generic metamorphosis takes place: the *comedia*, digesting the obstacles that García throws in its way ("puse impedimento en él," he self-consciously affirms) turns into a collection of tales—into something more like a novel. By introducing his narrative display texts and a specifically literary speech situation, García proclaims his own novelty and creates a new genre. Voltaire is not alone in thinking that this comedy of manners prefigures Molière.[13]

---

[12] Emilio Gómez Abreu, "Los graciosos en el teatro de Ruiz de Alarcón," *Investigaciones lingüísticas* (Mexico) III (1935), 189-201, notices that García performs many of the *gracioso's* ordinary functions, while Tristán, though nominally the *gracioso*, displays qualities associated normally with the protagonist.

[13] García perceives his situation in terms of contemporary legality. When "mi padre llegó... al tratarme el casamiento / puse impedimento en él," García's technical term is defined by E. de Echegaray, *Diccionario General Etimológico de la Lengua Española*, 3.778, as follows: "Cualquiera de las circunstancias que hacen ilícito o nulo el matrimonio." Clearly García's fictions are both delaying tactics and legal strategies. Pratt, 105, remarks that "storytelling... tends to establish its own turn-taking procedure such that if one speaker has been given the luxury of an uninterruptible turn, so should the others. Many of our earliest novel-like literary texts, such as those by Chaucer and Boccaccio, are such stories in series." This suggests that García pushes the genre in which he appears toward the novel. For the use

Like Said's exile, García believes that national or provincial limits
and customs only serve to constrain those who obey them. This much
emerges even in the curious little scene about the "cuello" or Dutch
collar. . Although this article of fashion serves to cover ruins and
ugliness, it also forces the wearer to curtail his freedom of movement:
"por no descomponerlo/se obliga a andar empalado" (275-6). If the
collars have this crucifying effect, observes Tristán, then why does
Don García wear just such a collar? García's resigned answer, "De
governar nos dexemos/el mundo," indicates in this important first
private conversation his awareness that even fictions do not inhabit
some Alexandrian universe remote from material human interests.[14]
His final comment in the play, "La mano doy, pues es fuerza," bears
out the early insight that a displaced author's fictions provide only
imaginary release from the reality of local authority.

Garcia's sense of his own strangeness gives him cause, then, to
invent his narratives. He attracts our sympathies because he wilfully
produces his difference, estrangement, and alien status in a manner
familiar to us from Joyce and Nabokov, from Hemingway and Fitz-
gerald, and even from the non-expatriate Nietzsche, who taught us to
mistrust tradition. That is to say, García repeatedly enters the role of
author—a role, paradoxically, that generally implies presence, authority, and solid identity. He even argues that his extravagant fables
provide a surer way to the truth. Tell me now, he challenges Jacinta,

> si esta mentira os admira,
> quando ha dicho esta mentira
> de mi afición la verdad (2053-55).

His love for truth drives him to embroider a world different *in toto*
from the world that confines him. Could we find a more succinct
credo for literary modernism?

---

of narrative insets and soliloquies in throttling straightforward, frontal plot
development in drama, see James L. Calderwood, *To Be and Not to Be: Negation
and Metadrama in Hamlet* (New York: Columbia University Press, 1983),
especially "Forms of Arrest: Scene, Inset, Soliloquy," 149-159, and *Shakes-
pearean Metadrama* (Minneapolis: University of Minnesota Press, 1971).
    [14] Edward W. Said, *The World, The Text, and The Critic* (Cambridge:
Harvard University Press, 1983), 31-53, argues that literary texts always
take on a circumstantial setting and remain inevitably worldly as critics
struggle over them in battles for interpretive power. "Texts of such a
length as *Tom Jones* aim to occupy leisure time of a quality not available to
just anyone. Moreover all texts essentially dislodge other texts or, more
frequently, take the place of something else" (45). Pratt, 115, seems to be
thinking along similar lines: "Far from being autonomous, self-contained,
self-motivating, context-free objects which exist independently from the
'pragmatic' concerns of 'everyday' discourse, literary works take place in a
context, and like any other utterance they cannot be described apart from
that context."

If García never quite shrugs off the Dutch collar and prescribed role that chafe him, his fictions liberate other characters from their stock roles and the *comedia* from its predictable formulae. Among the latter, "Yo soy quien soy," perhaps the hoariest of *comedia* conventions, provides the perfect illustration. As García recounts to Tristán the story of Juan's challenge and the ensuing duel, he says that he kept silent at the time because "el que no lo calla... quiere / que le estorven o le ayuden." He fully understands, that is, the conventions of silence that underwrite the *comedia* notion of honor—in, for example, *La estrella de Sevilla*, Don Sancho's silence demonstrates his possession of honor.

Having established García's mastery of the rituals of honor, the narrative proceeds with ever more Bobadillian extravagance to its climax: Don Juan's brains lying scattered on the ground. "But isn't this he right now?" exclaims Tristán. And in walks Don Juan. "¡Cosa estraña!" García replies smoothly, "Sin duda que le han curado / por ensalmo" (2786-7). Remembering that Sancho Panza blames the enchanters for bewitching Dulcinea, anyone knows by now that García's display text belongs to some mock-heroic genre and not to the romance (or the *comedia* of honor) at all.[15]

It is in this parodic context that we hear Don Juan produce the heroic formula: "Como quien soys lo avéys hecho." García instantly picks out his generic marker and repeats it, not once ("os doy palabra / como quien soy" [1803-4]) but twice ("como quien soy, no bolver / sino muerto o vitorioso" [1814-14]). Although Juan at first makes the error of assigning this episode to the epic mode ("es tan valiente que... diera a Alcides pesadumbre," he admires, confusing García with the very type of heroic virtue), Don Felis soon sets him straight, calling García's performance "mentira patente." By framing the *Yo soy quien soy* refrain in a literary narrative, the play gives the lie to the most venerable of *comedia* tropes. With his foreigner's sense of alternative worlds and contrapuntal dimensions, García simply cannot recognize himself in any static formula or statement of identity.

Having found sufficient cause for García's narrative display texts, we can turn to their consequences. García uses his tales to establish his identity. Louis Althusser has argued that ritual practices do indeed define each human subject, by which he means the apparently unified, responsible, and authorial self. Ideology, in Althusser's opinion,

has the function (which defines it) of "constituting" concrete individuals as subjects... When we recognize someone of our (pre-

---

15 For the comedia as a genre, see R. Menéndez Pidal, "Del honor en el teatro español," in *De Cervantes y Lope de Vega* (CA 120), 139-66, and A. Castro, "El drama de la honra en España y en su literatura," *Cuadernos* No. 38 (Sept.-Oct., 1959), 3-15 and No. 39 (Nov.-Dec., 1959), 16-28.

vious) acquaintance in the street, we show that we have recognized him (and have recognized that he has recognized us) by saying to him "hello, my friend" and shaking his hand (a material ritual practice of ideological recognition in everyday life...).[16]

"You and I are always already subjects," Althusser continues, "and as such constantly practice the rituals of ideological recognition." Alarcón's play does in fact offer substantial numbers of the rituals of recognition. They create significant anxiety for the central character, whose identity is somewhat adrift.

Narrative display texts—fictions—would appear to be García's defense against the "material practices of ideological recognition." Any request or question con constitute such a ritual:

> D. GARCIA ¡Don Juan de Sosa!
> D. JUAN   ¿Quién es?
> D. GARCIA ¿Ya olvidáys a don García?
> D. JUAN Veros en Madrid lo hazía,
>   y el nuevo trage (592-6).

Formerly a poor student and a second son wearing academic attire that promised the dubious status of a *letrado*, García now proves unrecognizable in the flashy garb that announces a courtier and first son. To his vertiginous sense that he, unlike the rest, has no stable identity, García responds by gleefully making up his own history. This he transmits by means of narrative display texts, which differ in important ways from other rituals of recognition.

For one thing, the literary speech situation treats imaginable rather than actual events and gives the speaker a considerable edge in the ongoing competition to gain the floor. "In ratifying a speaker's request to tell a story, we (the hearers) agree to allow him an enormous advantage in the competition for turns," M.L. Pratt observes.[17] We are obliged to keep quiet until the storyteller, with his narrative coda, gives up the floor. It is no surprise, then, that García only produces his tales in response to ratifying requests. After Juan's mutually embarrassing failure to recognize him, García remains on the scene, joining the conversation about a grand dinner:

> D. GARCIA ¿Música y cena, don Juan?
>   ¿Y anoche?
>   D. JUAN   Sí.

---

[16] Louis Althusser, "Ideology and Ideological State Apparatuses," in *Lenin and Philosophy and Other Essays*, trans. Ben Brewster (New York and London: Monthly Review Press, 1971), 127-193; quotation cited, 172.

[17] Pratt, 103-4, observes, "No wonder the potential narrator feels obliged to ask permission to make requests or to interrupt in contexts in which we do not have clear authority."

D. GARCIA   ¿Mucha cosa?
                   ¿Grande fiesta?
D. JUAN Assí es la fama.
D. GARCIA ¿Y muy hermosa la Dama?
D. JUAN Dízenme que es muy hermosa.
D. GARCIA ¡Bien!
D. JUAN   ¿Qué mysterios hazéys? (612-18).

Although Juan has plenty of chances to launch a tale of his own, he merely fills out the meter. García, after all, seems to know all about the dinner. Finally, García's monosyllabic "¡Bien!"—a marker that ordinarily truncates a conversational sequence—forces Juan's hand. He asks the question that authorizes García to elaborate an eighty-four line, uninterrupted narrative describing the supposed feast.

The narrator's role carries sizeable risks. In this way too it differs from other practices of ideological recognition. "In giving up floor fights, Audiences gain the right to pass judgment on the Speaker's contribution," Pratt explains. García seems to appreciate the jeopardy in which his author's role places him. "Contaréla," he reminds Juan, only "ya que veo/que os fatiga esse deseo." From the perspective of his audience, Jacinta fully understands that a narrator "is indebted to his audience for consenting to listen" (Pratt, 109):

D. GARCIA Pues, ¿qué ha alcanzado de vos
           El corazón que os he dado?
JACINTA El averos escuchado.
D. GARCIA Yo lo estimo (537-9).

In asserting his authority to impose narratives on others, García is also paradoxically accepting his subservience to their judgment.

That he is willing to accept a dependency which, in other respects, he shuns points to a third curious feature of the literary speech situation. Althusser notices that the rituals of recognition work below the level of consciousness to persuade the human subject that it "is the centre of its world, as a perceiving subject, as an active 'creative' subject, as a free subject and hence as responsible for its objects and their meaning" (238). The plurality of vision that goes along with García's role as a narrator makes him aware that this supposed autonomy is an illusion. The others suppose that home truths about identity can be flatly stated. "¿Soys indiano?" Jacinta demands. Although she merely wishes García to identify himself, her question enfolds a powerfully ideological component. The answer, in terms of propositional content, must be "no," but in García's own way he does at least resemble the stereotypic *indiano*: a suddenly fortunate upstart and second son arriving in Madird with fancy clothes but no manners. Garcia's evasive reply, that he has qualities associated with the *indiano*, sounds a metadramatic note, as does his parodic doubling of "yo soy quien soy." He seems at least tangentially aware that he is enacting a role on the Spanish stage. Jaime Concha has suggested that the self-portrayal reveals biographical aspects of Alarcón himself, "deforme, segundón, letrado, noble empobrecido, indiano."[18] Those who judge only the propositional content of García's stories leave no room for such partial, poetic truths.

Just as García himself imparts the contrapuntal awareness of other places, so his display texts include simultaneous dimensions. This suggests a fourth special feature of the literary speech situation—that narratives have many properties in common with written texts. They not only follow a controlled sequence from abstract to coda, but also are vulnerable to the suspicion and critical scrutiny normally reserved for writing. Jacinta, among others, discloses her marked preference for speech over writing. "El alma... quisiera ver con hablalle," she confides, thinking that only immediate speech will truly communicate García's character. Writing, by contrast, is incriminating. "Notorio verás tu error," she tells Lucrecia, "si adviertes que es el oír/cortesía, y admitir/ un papel claro favor." The *comedia* generally, as Elias Rivers has shown, treats writing as shameful; in *La estrella de Sevilla*, for instance, Busto rejects the king's *cédula*, for only the dishonorable have to back up their words with documents.[19]

When the ladies write a note, they prove how completely they accept the Platonic dichotomy, holding speech to be innocent and trustworthy but writing to be guilty and deceptive. Jacinta will not even put pen to paper and makes Lucrecia write in her stead. Neither woman signs the note: the bearer will *say* who has written ("le enseñará el portador"). García's narratives put to the rack this naive faith in the transparency of speech. When the unsigned note brings all three characters face to face, each mistakes the others' identities, motives, or both. Lucrecia concludes that Jacinta has double-crossed her; to disabuse her, Jacinta drops her pretence of being Lucrecia and pretends to be "a friend of Lucrecia." That is to say, by *pretending* to be what indeed she *is*, Jacinta is able to "prove" that García, who is now telling the truth, is lying. We have entered a Borgesian Labyrinth in

---

[18] Jaime Concha, "Introducción al teatro de Ruiz de Alarcón," *Ideologies and Literature*, vol. 2, no. 9 (1979), 36.

[19] Elias L. Rivers, "The Shame of Writing in *La Estrella de Sevilla*," *Folio*, No. 12 (June 1980), 105-17, analyzes the way writing is perceived to dishonor both writer and reader in one Siglo de Oro play. Oral commitments—giving one's word in a face-to-face encounter—offer the sole means by which honorable bonds might be established. The same author's *Quixotic Scriptures: Essays on the Textuality of Hispanic Literature* (Bloomington: Indiana University Press, 1983) places in a wider historical context the extremely complex negotiations between strictly rule-governed modes of written composition and the oral traditions that encroach upon it.

which speaking voices, the very guarantee of authenticity, create only more and more intricate fictions.

One consequence of García's display texts is, thus, to throw into chaos standard rituals of ideological recognition. The second is to make the others aware that they live in an ether comprised by repeatable formulae and antecedent texts. By Act III Tristán is quoting the Roman poets ("Virgilio dize" [2315] and "escrivió Marcial" [2295]). The old men have caught the trick of telling tales: "Mi padre está refiriendo/bien de espacio un cuento largo/a su tío" (1951-4), Lucrecia reports. But the most striking evidence that the world has become a text is the astonishing bulk of dialogue involving what can only be called textual analysis. Juan, as we have seen, tries to fit García into the tradition of Hercules but soon revises his reading: "Sus verdades serán/ya consejas para mí." Felis makes the same judgment on internal evidence alone, "porque tanta variedad/de tiendas, aparadores,/vaxillas de plata y oro" simply defy belief—"Esso un ciego lo vería" (1899).[20] Tristán, who proudly calls himself "secretario... del archivo" (2711-12), applies literary tools to even casual banter:

Y esta conjetura abona
más claramente, el negar
que era Lucrecia y tratar
luego en tercera persona... (2654-57).

As in so many places ordinary conversation here seems impenetrable to all but the most rigorous literary exegesis, replete with textual conjectures and discussions of shifts in voice.

García's intricate fables have taught the others that speech requires the same careful parsing accorded to texts. Part of the process involves generic identification: Jacinta only listens to him now, she says, as a tired businessman might amuse himself "en las fábulas de Ovidio." Juan reassigns his works, taking them from epic and placing them with *consejas*, old wives' tales. Although García has fulfilled Tristán's prophecy—"la fábula de la Corte/serás"—he has attained fame only in the humblest of genres. Jacinta tells him outright, "si otra vez os diere oído/... por divertirme ha sido." García cannot but realize that his efforts to stand out as an author have marginalized him all the more.

---

20 The archetypal oral mode, epic poetry that celebrates a hero who embodies a great national enterprise and foundation myth, is held up for gently ironic contemplation throughout the play. In the third scene, we find Tristán exclaiming, "¡Cierra, España!/que a César llevas contigo" (418-19). Coupled with the war cry of the *Reconquista* is "el polo de dinero," or Caesar, implying a degenerate time when money conquers all.

This is an unhappy consequence of producing display texts. Surely, in entering the role of author, García had aimed much higher. "Por ganar nombre," "tapar la boca" of every competitor, to excel those "quien solo el número aumenta" (856-8)—García has coveted the goals of every Renaissance artist. Yet now he finds the very audience he has taught to read, prepared to dismiss his performances as cheap farces. For example, he comes upon the two ladies, who are perusing, in the street, a letter he has written Lucrecia. As they busy themselves with textual analysis, García wonders why his Lucrecia should still be reading his note. "Por ventura lo repassa / regalándose con él," he ruefully suspects. Just as his epic formulae—"¡Aquí fue Troya!" he exclaims of the duel—turn in his mouth to mock-epic and travesty, here his signed marriage proposal serves (he suspects) as a joke. Even this most serious example of writing, affixing one's signature, the act by which subjects take on the most crushing repsonsibilities, has the status of fiction. Derrida makes the identical point. By signing his essay "Signature Event Context," he shows that serious and non-serious verbal performances are alike iterable, repeatable, and (in short) fictional events.

Although it might be possible to demonstrate the same parodic quality in García's other performances—his travelogue, his masque (the *cena*), his fabliau, replete with bedroom tricks and phallic pistol—these display narratives have a more important aspect affecting the third major theme of the play, that of time. García's arrival in Madrid disrupts a static, timeless world. There, the centuries revolve without changing a thing. At least so it seems to Isabel, who warns her long-betrothed mistress, "Advierte que siglos passas en vano" (1016-17). Tristán catalogues Madrid feminity as types of heavenly bodies stuck in an immutable firmament. Beltrán envisions the Corte as a sphere of unchanging values and the king as a sun constantly shining. García's narratives, far from introducing a Derridean element of undecidability and endless drift, propel this at-first static world into purposeful motion.

There is no doubt that García makes others acknowledge the existence of time. He wears a watch, for instance, and gives it crucial importance in his marriage fable. Centuries do not pass in vain for him; rather, "son ya siglos en mí / los instantes" (2690-91). He is often the subject of "nuevas" (1933) and he frequently summarizes the rapid changes he has induced:

que pienso que desvarío:
vine ayer y, en un momento,
tengo amor y casamiento
y causa de desafío (1752-55).

The paradox demands attention. Why should a speaker whose narratives might be expected to slow the dramatic tempo, actually speed things up? The answer lies in the nature of the texts that García produces, for in order to maintain his difference and yet establish his identity, he needs a new literary language.

A baroque aesthetic of potentiality and metamorphosis lay ready to hand. García's account of the *cena* by the river illustrates the unthought-of transmutations that art can work in nature. There, the opulence bordering on waste really does transform the brazen world into a golden one. Like the court masques it resembles, García's *cena* is "a lo italiano curiosa" and affords a banquet of the senses. "Olorosa" as "la región sabea," the event also addresses the taste-buds (with thirty-two plates, excluding dessert), the ear (with four *coros*), the eye (with enough torches to dim the stars), and even the skin (with enough artificial snow to rival the mountains). This baroque tour de force apprehends art in the act of improving nature: the musicians and dining tables lodge cunningly within a gigantic elm, the former (like Orpheus) taming their rude surroundings. The mistress overmatches the ivy with emeralds and sand with pearls and, as in another baroque masterpiece, Góngora's *Soledades* (I. 645-51), fireworks ("cohetes, bombas, y ruedas") bring down the whole region of fire. Thus García can truthfully claim that his display text "el artificio conserva" (720). His search for literary strategies that might overcome his sense of homelessness in Madrid might well end here, with an art that promises sweeping change.

A strangling creed of *mediocritas* opposes García's art of potentiality and extravagance. The *viejos* might well be expected to disparage all "estremos" (2983) or any "tal excesso" (3021) and to hold out for an art "más templada" (2982). Restrain yourself, counsels Beltrán: "juguéys contado/y habléys contadas razones," and above all, say little (1207-8). But to find the young women, who in comedy may claim recklessness as their birthright, advising the same prudence, suggests how ubiquitous the moderate course apparently is. "Quando esse límite excede," Jacinta sagely proclaims, "no se puede sufrir."

García of course refuses to give either rule to his conduct or restraint to his fictions. That he rejects *mediocritas* in behavior is clear enough. His most frequent epithets are "extremist" and "reckless," as in Tristan's thumbnail sketch:

Aquel hablar arrojado
mentir sin recato y modo;
aquel jactarse de todo
y hacerse en todo estremado (1245-48).

The same debate recurs on a more theoretical plane. In asserting that *el mentir* brings neither "gusto" nor "provecho," Beltrán denies in his son's fictions the qualities felt, in the Renaissance, to be indispensable to literature. Virtually all the tracts, commentaries, and defenses of poetry follow Horace in proclaiming that "the aim of the poet is to give profit or delight."[21] So does García: "Ya del mentir no dirá/que es sin gusto y sin provecho" (1734-5), he exclaims at one triumphal moment. Thus García defends his vice— with the very terms poets used to justify their art.

This fourth, theoretical dimension contains and explains the other three aspects of García's authorial role. The genesis of that role in his displacement, its consequence of establishing his identity as a narrator, and its wider effect of drawing others into the maelstrom of texts and transformations—all these resonate against the ground of contemporary theories of literature. Sir Philip Sidney, to take just one internationally-known theorist, had helped to make widely current the notion that "the poets' persons and doings are but pictures what should be, and not stories what have been."[22] This art of the possible was not limited strictly to literary texts, either. Humanist poetics allowed for *historia conficta*, as well.[23] Ariosto and Tasso, for example, were thought to have distorted facts but nonetheless retained "truth to pattern"; Roland may not have existed but Europe's wars on Islam certainly had.[24] In speech-act theory this more generous sense of truth extends to individual utterances. Walter Cerf comments that the very idea of a speech *act* is "dialectically related to the concept of the potential." Austin himself only wishes to "stimulate our wretched imaginations," as he

---

[21] Horace, *Epistle to Piso*, trans. Walter Jackson Bate, "The Art of Poetry," in *Criticism: The Major Texts* (New York: Harcourt, Brace, & Co., 1952), 56.

[22] Sir Philip Sidney, *A Defence of Poetry*, in *Miscellaneous Prose of Sir Philip Sidney* ed. Katherine Duncan-Jones and Jan Van Dorsten (Oxford: Clarendon, 1973), 85.

[23] Sidney, 90-91: "I conclude, therefore, that he excelleth history, not only in furnishing the mind with knowledge, but in setting it forward to that which deserveth to be called and accounted good...."

[24] John R. Beverley, "History and Poetic Myth," in *Aspects of Gongora's 'Soledades'* (Amsterdam: John Benjamins, B.V., 1980), 83-102, traces the doctrine of *historia conficta* back to Aristotle's *Poetics*, in which the poet describes "not what has actually happened but the kind of thing that *should* happen (have happened)." Beverley contends that the "patriotic epic and epic hero *per se*" were "no longer a genuine possibility" amid the "growing sense of crisis and decadence in Spain"; the "exhaustion in Renaissance epic and pastoral" led to the novel and "a strategy of invention of a *possible* discourse when all models and canons have suddenly become obsolete." This rhetoric of potentiality informs *La Verdad Sospechosa*, I would suggest, as much as it does Góngora's *Soledades* or *Don Quixote*.

says, in order to show that if meaning is context bound, that context nonetheless is boundless.[25]

García manifestly believes in the capacity of his display texts to do things with words. This confidence is bound up with his acute awareness of time: "Quando lo sepan," he remarks of one fiction he imposes on the ladies, "avré ganado en su casa/o en su pecho ya las puertas/con esse medio" (822-4). This belief in the sovereign power of the creating intellect allies García to Donne, Marino, Góngora, and others, whose sense of multiple dislocated planes leads them, as well, to posit an alienated but unifying authorial intelligence. García, like them, assumes that texts exist to provoke wonder or *admiración*.[26] He intends to fashion his dinner-narrative in such a way that "a las romanas y griegas/fiestas que al mundo admiraron/nueva admiración pusiera" (768-70). "Admiración" serves in this way to advance his own stories or versions expressly against the stories and visions proposed by others. You cannot imagine how sweet it is, he tells Tristán, "quando llega un portanuevas/muy orgulloso a contar/una hazaña o una fiesta/taparle la boca yo/con otra tal, que se buelva/con sus nuevas en el cuerpo" (846-51). To monopolize turn-taking with a display text is, at the local level as it were, to promote one's particular poetic vision in an alien world.

A sense of one's estrangement, interacting with the literary strategies one deploys to reaffirm one's identity, dialectically issues in a peculiarly time-bound sort of narrative art. García imagines the narrator as a *portanuevas*; defeated competitors go away with their own *nuevas* still locked up in their breasts. Although "display texts can be introduced into conversation rather easily" and "do not have to relate in any strict logical or topical way to prior discourse," says Pratt, "News in conversation has an even greater freedom of occurrence." In fact, "news can be volunteered at almost any moment when the floor is up for grabs" and is "the device we most commonly use for establishing topics of conversation in situations where the topic is not predefined."[27] This principle explains, in part,

---

25 Walter Cerf, critical review of *How To Do Things With Words*, quoted in Norris, *Deconstructive Turn*, 81. J. L. Austin, "Performative Utterances," in *Philosophical Papers*, ed. J. O. Urmson and G. L. Warnock (Oxford and New York: Oxford University Press, 1979, 3rd ed.), 184; quoted in Shoshana Felman, *The Literary Speech Act: Don Juan with J. L. Austin, or Seduction in Two Languages*, trans. Catherine Porter (Ithaca, New York: Cornell University Press, 1983), 116.

26 James V. Mirollo, *The Poet of the Marvelous: Giambattista Marino* (New York and London: Columbia University Press, 1963), for example, discusses the manner in which an aesthetic principle of *wonder* migrated from Mannerist theories of painting into the poetics of the Baroque.

27 Pratt, 144-5.

why García tells lies rather than jokes, anecdotes, novellas, or epic poems. Since news is supposed to have actually occurred, it obtains priority over other narrative display texts.

García's wish to efface his estrangement, defend his identity, and overwhelm his audience, entices him irresistibly to present his display texts as news. The dynamics controlling the literary speech situation guarantee the floor to a reporter of news and therefore encourage García to lie. But the exile has also a special need not to be overpowered by the world around him. He may gloat over those who know just one world or one truth: "!Qué fácil en creer/el que no sabe mentir!" He must go beyond the facts around him. Don Juan mistakenly supposes that García merely is reporting those facts: "¡Por Dios, que la avéys pintado/de colores tan perfectas,/que no trocara en oyrla/ por averme hallado en ella." Tristán begs to correct him. García's narrative does not imitate but rather surpasses the facts: "pueda/pintar un combite tal/que la verdad misma venza." The local narrator of conversational display texts apparently possesses the same sovereign freedom that Sidney confers on poets, who are not "tied to the truth of a foolish world."

García lies not merely because presenting "news" is the one sure way to get the floor, but also to prosecute his sense of his own difference from a society that treats him as a stranger. He feels that he must either get his own story out, or accept the standard story.[28] He insists that the complacent Madrileños shall never reduce *him* to gaping *admiración*: "Fingílo, porque me pesa/que piense nadie que hay cosa/que mover mi pecho pueda/a invidia o admiración" (837-40). Explaining himself, he adds

> Que admirarse es ignorancia,
> como imbidiar ès baxeza (838-43)

This bit of Horatian stoicism—*nil admirari*—comes strangely yoked to a baroque aesthetic of the marvelous. García constructs his fables, apparently, in order to demystify what others say and to avert the confusing passions that Horace condemns. We are left with the final paradox that García lies from explicitly ethical motives.

---

[28] Stanley Fish, "How to Do Things with Austin and Searle," 1019, develops Strawson's notion that a *standard story* establishes what it means to mean within an interpretive community. "What I have been suggesting is that identification (or specification of facts) is *always* within a story. Some stories, however, are more prestigious than others; and one story is always the standard one, the one that presents itself as uniquely true and is, in general, so accepted. Other, non-standard, stories will of course continue to be told, but they will be regarded as non-factual, when, in fact, they will only be non-authorized." García consciously attempts to replace the standard story, *la verdad*, with his non-standard story, *la mentira*.

It would be fair to say that Alarcón's play is at least in part an extended inquiry into the nature and ethics of the literary speech situation. That situation belongs among other practices of ideological recognition; it is not an hermetic, Alexandrian world but rather one that involves the real interests of speaker/narrators and hearer/audiences. It fixes their reciprocal duties (to entertain and to attend), prescribes their intervals of speech and silence, distributes their rights (the speaker's to elaborate "de espacio" and without fear of interruption, the hearers' right to judge the resulting performance). But unlike many practices of ideological recognition, which reinforce existing social identities, the literary speech situation organizes human relationships anew. By convention the author knows more than his audience and by definition assumes authority over them. Thus he can utter exercitives and declaratives, which not only advocate what should be but also ensure that, for a narrator and audience so defined, what ought to be, is.

The problem of the play is a problem affecting baroque aesthetics generally. Just as Sidney defends a poetry of the possible, which makes the brazen world golden; just as Góngora and Cervantes discover a language able to transofrm reality (if only the reality of literary tradition); just as the inventors of masques create mythical roles that courtiers can take over the line separating masquers from spectators, so also García's narrative fictions transform the realities *comedia* usually accepts. The "yo soy quien soy" formula cannot survive García's dueling narrative except as a parody; the *comedia de enredo* finds a parodic double in his Salamanca fabliau; the stock roles of *segundón, indiano,* and *gracioso,* or of noble *caballero* and honorable father, emerge strangely different after entering García's literary speech situation. And García himself successfully authors his own identity and marriage, even if they are not the ones he intends.[29]

---

[29] "From the way history misunderstands itself stems the performance of revolutions," says Marx; "The revolution of 1848 knew no better than to parody at some points 1789 and at others the revolutionary traditions of 1793-5. In the same way, the beginner who has learned a new language always retranslates it into his mother tongue; he can only be said to have appropriated the spirit of the new language and to be able to express himself in it freely when he can manipulate it without reference to the old, and when he forgets his original language while using the new one." Karl Marx, *Der Achtzehnt Brumaire des Louis Bonaparte* (Berlin: Dietz Verlag, 1947), 8; trans. Ben Fowkes in Marx, *Surveys from Exile,* ed. David Fernbach (London: Pelican Books, 1973), 144; quoted in Said, *World, Text, and Critic,* 123. The transcendental homelessness that Lukács calls the defining characteristic for the modern novel, would seem to characterize García's imaginative projections of himself to the Indies, Salamanca, and the Manzanares, as well as his (failing) efforts to discover a new possible discourse when all the

Vico's premise that "men make their own history, but not the one they wish" might be said to inform *La Verdad Sospechosa*. Nietzsche points out that "truth is nothing but the solidification of old metaphors"; Alarcón demonstrates the corollary, that to destroy old metaphors means to destroy the truth.[30] The literary speech situation frames and distances all the old clichés—manners, morality, stock roles and poetic diction; seen at arm's length, these appear uncomfortably artificial. Alone among the practices of ideological recognition, the author-audience relationship foregrounds its own origins: an audience that consents to take for truth what an author imagines and constructs.

Historically, the Spanish intelligentsia was mourning a similar decay of the old metaphors. Part of the general *declinación* was the degeneration of language. "La elegancia de Garcilaso, que ayer tuvo por osadía poética, hoy es prosa vulgar": this instance of decline, from Jerónimo de San José, only epitomizes the much wider drift from Imperial epic to vulgar farce.[31] García's baroque illusions, by their very refulgence, bring into view the fictional origins of Spain's heroic past, a truth that much other *comedia* leaves unsuspected.

---

available models have become obsolete. García's distance from his own topographical and linguistic origins make him a precursor of later, more fully developed novelistic heroes.

[30] *The New Science of Giambattista Vico*, trans. Thomas Goddard Bergin and Max Harold Frisch (Ithaca, New York: Cornell University Press, 1968), 425: "It is true that men have themselves made this world of nations... but this world without doubt issued from a mind often diverse, at times quite contrary, and always superior to the particular ends that men had proposed to themselves... Men mean to gratify their bestial lust and abandon their offspring, and they inaugurate the chastity of marriage from which families arise," etc. From Vico's unique scheme for reconciling determinism and free will, Marx drew his own principle that "men make their own history, but not just as they please." Alarcón intuits a similarly roundabout ruse of reason, I think, by having García's outrages work themselves into wholly conventional acts of writing that reinforce and perpetuate the Madrid society that he attempts to buck.

[31] Jeronimo de San José quoted in Malcolm K. Read, "A Linguistic Perspective on the Town/Country debate in the Spanish Renaissance," *Journal of Hispanic Philology* 1 (1977), 201. The theory that language had degenerated from its primitive roots (exemplified for Huarte de San Juan by Christ's language) was balanced by a theory of cyclic improvement, Read points out. Robles considers peasant language "lo mismo que los brutos... no hace en ello más que lo que el caballo relinchando." The peasant's incapacity to *write* actually excluded him, according to Robles, from the human community. For the widespread feeling among Spanish writers and court official that "se va todo a fondo—'the ship is going down'," see J. H. Elliott, "Self-perception and Decline in Early Seventeenth-Century Spain," *Past and Present* 74, 41-61.

García's *embelecos* and embroideries have a certain resonance for modern critics as well, if only because our own culture and literature proclaim the nagging ache of exile from origin, home, and tradition. One of the hardiest of all our nostalgias is the same one that the Madrileños exhibit, the yearning for a speaking voice unobstructed by writing. Alarcón gaily puts the myth of a full speaking presence to the torch. Speech in his play models itself around literary forms: Don Juan shapes his around *capa y espada* plays and romance; the ladies, around the *comedia de enredo*; Don Beltrán, around the honor play and the prose genre of advice to a son. But effective speech in each case follows writing. Thus even the Spanish *comedia*, which in Lope's and others' hands comes so close to the style of oral composition described in Albert Lord's *The Singer of Tales*, cannot on Alarcón's evidence provide us with plenitude, full presence, and Edenic orality.[32] Alarcón's own slightly eccentric position, just outside the quartet of major Golden Age dramatists, makes him in this way a dangerous supplement indeed.

Marymount College of Kansas

---

[32] Albert B. Lord, *The Singer of Tales* (Cambridge: Harvard University Press, 1960).

Power Plays in
La casa de Bernarda Alba

JANIS OZIMEK-MAIER

HE ACTION of *La casa de Bernarda Alba*, by Federico García Lorca, centers on a world which is dominated and controlled by the tyrannical figure of Bernarda Alba, and in which behavior is both manipulated and codified by the central character. It is Bernarda who has determined the parameters of her world: she has decided whom her daughters may or may not marry, which image of her family shall be projected to the outside world, and—above all—she has determined that her inner domain shall not be penetrated. This exclusionary attitude is evident on a number of occasions in the play. During the gathering following her husband's funeral, for example, the male guests are told to remain on the exterior patio while the female guests sip lemonade inside. But even this limited amount of contact with the outside world is unacceptable to Bernarda, for as the women leave she remarks: "¡Andar a vuestras casas a criticar todo lo que habéis visto!... Ojalá tardéis muchos años en pasar el arco de mi puerta!" (*Obras completas*, p. 1450). In addition, Bernarda makes reference to the long-standing traditions and social attitudes which govern her life, and, as a result, the lives of the other members of her family: "En ocho años que dure el luto no ha de entrar en esta casa el viento de la calle. Hacemos cuenta que hemos tapiado con ladrillos puertas y ventanas. Así pasó en casa de mi padre y en casa de mi abuelo" (p. 1451).

Bernarda recognizes no opinion or viewpoint other than her own, an attitude which elicits various different reactions on the part of others: intimidation, anger, frustration, and, ultimately, rebellion. The result is a series of power plays in which language is used as a manipulative tool. Through her linguistic relationship with the members of her family, Bernarda attempts to control their lives, to circumscribe their existence, by imposing her own system of values on them and by eliminating those elements which she perceives as threats to her authority. But it is also by linguistic means that the members of Bernarda's family respond to her tyranny and to her attempts to force them to live a hermetic existence. La Poncia, Bernarda's long-time housekeeper, attempts to usurp the authority of her mistress by expressing her own opinions regarding the manner in which Bernarda's household should be run, and by assuming a position of dominance over the maid and over Adela, Bernarda's rebellious daughter. Furthermore Adela, whose passion for Pepe el Romano forces a wedge between him and her sister Angustias, and María Josefa, the mad grandmother, reject Bernarda's authoritarian rule and values in favor of personal freedom. As we shall see, in all of these instances language is used not only as a tool for communication—for in point of fact the communicative process breaks down in the course of Bernarda's efforts to establish and maintain control of her world—but as a source of power, indeed as a weapon used both offensively and defensively.

The opening minutes of the play focus on La Poncia and the maid, who are busy preparing the house for a gathering following the burial of Bernarda's husband. Bernarda does not appear on stage for quite some time, which leaves La Poncia free to express her opinions regarding her mistress and (for the benefit of the spectator) to reveal verbally the hierarchical relationship which exists not only between her and Bernarda, but also between her and the maid. La Poncia reveals a multiplicity of attitudes toward her mistress. On the one hand, she appears to be intimidated by Bernarda, as we see in her orders to the maid to clean the house well prior to Bernarda's return: "¡Ya viene! Limpia bien todo. Si Bernarda no ve relucientes las cosas me arrancará los pocos pelos que me quedan... ¡Limpia; limpia ese vidriado!" (p. 1441). But at the same time she reveals her devious, manipulative nature in taking food from Bernarda's coffers for the maid and for herself when Bernarda is away, making certain that the lock is replaced so that her covert action will not be detected. Both of these attitudes on the part of La Poncia, furthermore, are counterbalanced by the contempt which she feels for Bernarda, as she indicates to the maid:

¡Quisiera [Bernarda] que ahora como no come ella, que todas nos muriéramos de hambre! ¡Mandona! ¡Dominanta!... Tirana de todos los que la rodean. Es capaz de sentarse encima de tu corazón y ver cómo te mueres durante un año sin que se le cierre esa sonrisa fría que lleva en su maldita cara... Ella, la más aseada; ella, la más decente; ella, la más alta. ¡Buen descanso ganó su pobre marido! (pp. 1440-41).

The relationship which exists between la Poncia and the maid, on the other hand, is one of unilateral authority. La Poncia gives the maid a series of orders which the latter neither opposes nor questions, and she demonstrates her position of authority over the maid by deciding that it is appropriate to give the woman a handful of garbanzo beans, adding that because of the events of the day Bernarda will not notice the missing food. The maid, in turn, exerts authority over the "mendiga," who comes begging for food scraps. Having claimed the food for herself, the maid wastes no time in expelling the woman and her child from the house: "Fuera de aquí. ¿Quién os dijo que entraseis? Ya me habéis dejado los pies señalados" (p. 1444). What we have, then, is a hierarchical relationship of power which may be summarized as follows:

BERNARDA : LA PONCIA : LA CRIADA : LA MENDIGA

From the preceding exchanges the spectator receives a mental image of Bernarda as the dominant figure of the household, and our sense is that, while Bernarda is not necessarily respected, she is certainly obeyed. We are not at all surprised, therefore, when upon her entrance in Act I Bernarda utters the exercitive[1] "¡Silencio!", nor are we unprepared for the frequent directives which characterize her statements to her daughters and to La Poncia following her appearance on stage. It quickly becomes apparent, however, that what we had initially perceived as authority on the part of Bernarda is in reality merely power,[2] for Bernarda fails to command the full respect of her family, and her mandates are neither accepted nor followed by all. Her world is closed, but not hermetic.

On two separate occasions La Poncia attempts to usurp Bernarda's power by asserting her own authority, and in both instances Bernarda strikes an immediate counter-blow. In Act I of the play La Poncia remarks, in reference to the uneven distribution of the inheritance, "¡Cuánto dinero le queda a Angustias!... Y a las otras, bastante menos," to which Bernarda replies angrily, "Ya me lo has dicho tres veces y no te he querido replicar" (p. 1468). In Act II La Poncia again attempts to express her opinion concerning the state of affairs in Bernarda's house, noting "¿A ti no te parece que Pepe estaría mejor

---

[1] "Exercitives," as defined by J. L. Austin, are a class of utterances which constitute the exercising of powers, rights, or influence. Examples are appointing, voting, urging, advising, and warning. See Austin, *How To Do Things With Words*.

[2] I base this distinction between power and authority on the fact that the latter is contractual whereas the former is not. That is, if the parties involved do not recognize a voice of authority, then the effect of that voice is potentially nullified. Where power is concerned, on the other hand, there is the possibility of coercion.

casado con Martirio o..., ¡sí!, con Adela?... A mí me parece mal que
Pepe esté con Angustias..." (p. 1500). Bernarda's retort dulls the
point of La Poncia's blade with a swift thrust of the verbal sword:
"¡Ya estamos otra vez!... Te deslizas para llenarme de malos sueños.
Y no quiero entenderte..." (p. 1500). Bernarda's response in both
cases may be explained by means of the Doctrine of the "Infelicities,"
in accordance with J. L. Austin's Speech-Act model.[3] As Austin
indicates, one of the necessary conditions for the smooth functioning
of a performative[4] is that "the particular persons and circumstances in
a given case must be appropriate for the invocation of the particular
procedure invoked" (Austin, p. 34), and that a failure of said condition
will void the attempted performative. In the cited exchanges between
La Poncia and Bernarda there is a misinvocation of procedure, for
within the hierarchical value system established by Bernarda she
herself is the only person who possesses the right to pass judgment,
impose rules and make decisions. Despite La Poncia's age and the fact
that she has been in Bernarda's household for thirty years, she is
nevertheless a servant. As such, she lacks the right to make judg-
mental statements in matters of direct concern to Bernarda. As the
latter tells La Poncia at one point, "Eso es lo que debías hacer. Obrar y
callar a todo. Es la obligación de los que viven a sueldo" (p. 1500).

Bernarda's retorts to La Poncia—"No te he querido replicar" and
"No quiero entenderte"—thus have the effect of undercutting La
Poncia's words and, as a result, of voiding the attempted power
struggle. Through her words Bernarda has redefined the hierarchy
which separates her from the others, in this instance La Poncia, has
reminded La Poncia of the fact that she lacks authority, and has
reiterated her refusal to recognize any rules, conventions or opinions
other than her own. But what must be emphasized here is the fact
that La Poncia's attempts to transcend her role as servant clearly place
Bernarda on the defensive. Recognizing the need to protect the
integrity of her domain and sensing that there are cracks in the
foundation of her strong-hold,[5] Bernarda feels threatened by La

---

   [3] The Doctrine of the "Infelicities" is the doctrine of the things that can
be and go wrong on the occasion of making an utterance.

   [4] A "performative" is an utterance which indicates that the issuing of
the utterance is the performing of an action. Examples are "I bet," "I declare
war," and "I name this ship the Queen Elizabeth."

   [5] By the second act of the play Bernarda has begun to realize that one of
her daughters has been seeing Pepe secretly, which threatens to dishonor
her family by providing the townspeople with a new source of gossip. In
addition, she has begun to sense the antagonistic relationship among her
daughters, a concern which is intensified by La Poncia's suggestion that the
situation is more serious than she suspects ("Bernarda, aquí pasa una cosa
muy grande...") and that Bernarda is blind to the truth of the matter.
Furthermore, the effect of the outside world has been felt within the walls

Poncia's words. On a number of additional occasions in the course of Act II she negates her housekeeper's assertions, thereby further undermining the latter's attempts to assume a position of authority. In speaking of Angustias, for example, Bernarda says that she must be married immediately to Pepe el Romano, so as to eliminate the conflict with Adela. La Poncia concurs with Bernarda's statement, noting, "Claro; hay que retirarla de aquí," to which Bernarda replies angrily: "No a ella. ¡A él!" (p. 1496). Another example occurs in this same scene, as La Poncia continues to agree with Bernarda: "Claro. A él hay que alejarlo de aquí. Piensas bien" (p. 1496). Bernarda's retort is swift and clear: "No pienso. Hay cosas que no se pueden ni se deben pensar. Yo ordeno" (p. 1496). One final case in which Bernarda reveals the defensive nature of her struggle to retain control occurs in this same scene, as she and La Poncia continue their verbal jousting. In discussing the disappearance of Pepe's photo and the fact that Martirio said that her taking it was a joke, Bernarda says: "Después de todo, ella dice que ha sido una broma. ¿Qué otra cosa puede ser?" La Poncia replies, suggesting devious behavior on the part of Martirio, "¿Tú lo crees así?" which prompts Bernarda to counter arrogantly with: "No lo creo. ¡Es así!" (pp. 1497-8).

Thus on a number of occasions Bernarda has felt herself under attack by La Poncia, and she has responded accordingly. But her authority is also opposed by Adela, who ignores the fact that Angustias has been chosen to marry Pepe el Romano. From a point early in the play it is apparent that Adela rejects the rules of Bernarda's world, as evidenced by the fact that when Bernarda asks for a fan, Adela gives her one with a bright floral design. Bernarda's response is explosive: she hurls the brightly-colored fan to the ground, saying emphatically, "¿Es éste el abanico que se da a una viuda? Dame uno negro y aprende a respetar el luto de tu padre" (p. 1451). This exchange between Bernarda and Adela is of great importance in the play, not only because it communicates visually Adela's defiance and the conflict of values which separates the two characters,[6] but also

of Bernarda's fortress: Bernarda's daughters and María Josefa have begun to show signs of unrest; La Poncia's illicit tales have sparked their interest in the activities of the outside world; Bernarda's daughters echo the songs sung by the workers as they return from the fields at night; and the presence of Pepe's photo has served as a catalyst for the discord, jealousy and animosity within the family.

6 The bright floral pattern of Adela's fan has a parallel in the flowers which María Josefa wears in her hair and on her breast as she speaks of her desire to marry, and in the story of Paca "la Roseta," who was carried off one night and returned the following day wearing "una corona de flores en la cabeza" (p. 1456). Equally significant is the fact that, while her mother and sisters conform to the doctrine of mourning by wearing black, Adela expresses her desire to wear a green dress. By projecting these images

because it serves to underscore Bernarda's attitudes with regard to her "subjects." In asking for a fan, Bernarda says one thing but implies another: she says "Niña, dame el abanico," but means to say "Dame un abanico negro." The conversational implicature of Bernarda's words is clear: she believes that using a black fan is required in a house of mourning, and she expects the members of her household to follow her maxims. Therefore, by using the definite article "el" rather than the indefinite article "un" she has communicated her assumption that Adela will comply with the established rules of acceptability. When Adela fails to do so, Bernarda is forced to clarify her demand by eliminating the illocutionary ambiguity of her previous statement. In so doing, she reiterates to her rebellious daughter her value system and her expectations regarding social norms: "Dame uno negro y aprende a respetar el luto de tu padre."

It is clear, then, that the ambiguity of Bernarda's words stems from the clash of two worlds, with their respective value systems, conventions and ideals. But the question arises as to whether Bernarda's illocutionary ambiguity is intentional or not. We are unfortunately unable to rely upon the text for illumination regarding this point, for the stage directions are unclear as to the precise location of the floral fan: is it visible, as on a table, or is it out of sight, for instance in the pocket of Adela's dress? As a result of this lack of clarity in the stage directions the reader (rather than the spectator, since in the production of the play the director would be forced to make a decision)is somewhat confused as to the nature of Bernarda's intention. If she does not see the fan prior to her mandate, the resultant ambiguity would be considered unintentional, the product of her assumption that the members of her family share her value system and accept the rules of her totalitarian regime. In that case, Bernarda's words to Adela would carry no implication other than the fact that she is intolerant and egocentric. If prior to her mandate she does see the fan, on the other hand, the ambiguity of her directive would be considered intentional and, consequently, the Cooperative Principle would be violated. Specifically, there would be a violation of the maxim of Manner, which states that for the communicative process to be effective the speaker must avoid ambiguity and obscurity.[7] As a result, if Bernarda has in fact violated the Cooperative

---

against a black and white background, Lorca has—in typically Ibsenian fashion—used the flowers and bright colors as a verbal or visual counterpoint to the austerity of Bernarda's dominion.

[7] In defining the Cooperative Principle, H. P. Grice states: "Make your conversational contribution such as is required, at the stage at which it occurs, by the accepted purpose or direction of the talk exchange in which you are engaged." See Grice, "Logic and Conversation," p. 45.

Principle, her attitude toward Adela could be seen as deliberately confrontational and antagonistic.

But regardless of whether the ambiguity of Bernarda's words is intentional or involuntary, what emerges from this exchange is a sense of conflict, a power play between two individuals who are struggling to assert themselves and to define the boundaries of their worlds. Adela has made a strong personal statement, one which does not coincide with Bernarda's philosophy and which underscores a basic lack of understanding between the two characters. With the brightly-colored fan, as in the case of her expressed desire to wear a green dress, Adela strikes a rebellious chord in a house of supposed purity and mourning, rebelling against the authoritarian rule and intolerance of her mother, and against the condemnation of an oppressive society.

However, Bernarda is not the only figure whose presence denies Adela the possibility of personal freedom, love and sexual fulfillment. Her sisters and La Poncia, who attempt to thwart her nightly encounters with Pepe el Romano, pose equally strong threats. Martirio, in particular, monitors Adela's every move and takes every available opportunity to remind her of the fact that she has over-stepped the bounds of morality and decency. It is Martirio who quickly offers Bernarda a black fan after the latter has angrily rejected Adela's brightly-colored one, and it is Martirio who suggests to Adela that she dye her green dress black. Likewise, in an attempt to preserve the purity and honor of the family—and to satisfy her own feelings of jealousy—Martirio vows that she will keep Adela and Pepe el Romano apart at all costs:

> ¡Adela!... ¡Deja a ese hombre!... No es ese el sitio de una mujer honrada... Ha llegado el momento de que yo hable. Esto no puede seguir así... Ese hombre sin alma vino por otra. Tú te has atravesado... Yo no permitiré que lo arrebates. El se casará con Angustias (p. 1526).

Martirio's pledge to limit Adela's freedom by controlling her indecent behavior reaches tragic proportions at the end of the play, when she gives Adela to believe that Pepe has been fatally wounded by Bernarda's shotgun. By deliberately lying to Adela, Martirio has attempted to assume a position of power over her younger sister. She has exerted control over the destiny of another in much the same way as she herself has been restrained by Bernarda, although the consequences of her words in this instance are far more grave: Adela's response to the supposed death of her lover is her ultimate rebellion in the form of suicide.

La Poncia also monitors Adela's every move and, like Martirio, she takes every opportunity to confront Adela with the indecency of her

thoughts and actions, thereby serving as the voice of conscience.
When accused by Adela of meddling in the affairs of others and of
seeing more than she should, La Poncia responds,

> Las viejas vemos a través de las paredes. ¿Dónde vas de noche
> cuando te levantas?... ¿Por qué te pusiste casi desnuda con la luz
> encendida y la ventana abierta al pasar Pepe el segundo día que
> vino a hablar con tu hermana?... ¡Deja en paz a tu hermana, y si
> Pepe el Romano te gusta, te aguantas!... Sombra tuya he de ser
> (pp. 1480-1).

At the same time, La Poncia is an extension of Bernarda, many of
whose values and obsessions she shares. Despite her feeling that
Bernarda should be more lenient with her daughters, La Poncia is
nevertheless offended by indecency and immorality, and she considers
it her duty to ensure that Bernarda's household is protected from
both. As she tells Adela, "¡Velo! Para que las gentes no escupan al
pasar por esta puerta... No os tengo ley a ninguna, pero quiero vivir
en casa decente. ¡No quiero mancharme de vieja!" (pp. 1481-2).

In La Poncia's opinion, Adela must be separated from Pepe el
Romano so that he may be permitted to marry Angustias, and she
makes every effort to convince Adela of the destructive nature of her
actions. The result is a power play in which each attempts to assert
her will and to demonstrate a greater degree of emotional and
psychological fortitude than the other:

> ADELA Es inútil tu consejo. Ya es tarde. No por encima de
> ti, que eres una criada; por encima de mi madre
> saltaría para apagarme este fuego que tengo levan-
> tado por piernas y boca. ¿Qué puedes decir de mí?
> ¿Que me encierro en mi cuarto y no abro la puerta?
> ¿Que no duermo? ¡Soy más lista que tú! Mira a ver
> si puedes agarrar la liebre con tus manos.

> LA PONCIA No me desafíes, Adela, no me desafíes. Porque yo
> puedo dar voces, encender luces y hacer que toquen
> las campanas.

> ADELA Trae cuatro mil bengalas amarillas y ponlas en las
> bardas del corral. Nadie podrá evitar que suceda lo
> que tiene que suceder.

> LA PONCIA ¡Tanto te gusta ese hombre!

> ADELA ¡Tanto! Mirando sus ojos me parece que bebo su
> sangre lentamente.

LA PONCIA Yo no te puedo oír.

ADELA ¡Pues me oirás! Te he tenido miedo. ¡Pero ya soy más fuerte que tú! (p. 1482).

This exchange brings to light various important elements. In the first place, it reveals a realization on Adela's part of the fact that she has done nothing wrong and that her passion will enable her to triumph over all who oppose her. Likewise, Adela's reference to the fact that La Poncia is a maid reveals an awareness of class distinctions which renders La Poncia's warnings to her entirely ineffective. But above all, La Poncia's words—"Yo no te puedo oír"—are clearly reminiscent of Bernarda's retorts to La Poncia—". . . no te he querido replicar" and "no quiero entenderte"—when the latter attempts to voice authority. Despite the fact that it is La Poncia who serves as a link to the outside world, through the tales which she recounts to Bernarda's daughters of life beyond the confines of their cloistered existence, she is clearly offended by Adela's expression of passion. Adela's words represent a threat to the integrity and decency of Bernarda's household, both of which are ideals which La Poncia shares with her mistress, and it is this perceived threat that prompts her refusal to hear what Adela is saying. Although on numerous occasions La Poncia clashes with Bernarda, she is nonetheless in many respects like her mistress, a fact confirmed by her words to Magdalena: "Yo tengo la escuela de tu madre" (p. 1477).

Adela is thus surrounded by individuals who seek to dominate and control her: Bernarda, Martirio, La Poncia, and also Angustias and Magdalena, all are offended and threatened by her involvement with Pepe el Romano and, in the case of her sisters, are jealous of her happiness. But Adela refuses to be confined and repressed, just as she will not resign herself to the passive, death-in-life existence which her sisters have dutifully accepted. When Magdalena suggests to her that she accustom herself to a life of mourning and solitude, for example, Adela replies: "No me acostumbraré. Yo no puedo estar encerrada. No quiero que se me pongan las carnes como a vosotras; no quiero perder mi blancura en estas habitaciones; mañana me pondré mi vestido verde y me echaré a pasear por la calle. ¡Yo quiero salir!" (p. 1466). Unlike the speech of her sisters, which reveals a generally submissive and non-aggressive attitude throughout the play, Adela's language may be characterized as being forceful, direct and at times hostile. Her speech is marked by a prevalence of commissives and directives,[8] two classifications of illocutionary acts which contribute to this sense of fortitude and dominance, as exemplified by her words to Martirio:

---

[8] As defined by Mary Louise Pratt, "commissives are illocutionary acts that commit the speaker to doing something, for example, promising,

¡Déjame ya! ¡Durmiendo o velando, no tienes por qué meterte en lo
mío! ¡Yo hago con mi cuerpo lo que me parece!... ¡Quisiera ser
invisible, pasar por las habitaciones sin que me preguntarais dónde
voy!... ¡No me mires más!... No me deja respirar... Mi cuerpo
será de quien yo quiera... Pepe el Romano es mío... Seré lo que él
quiera que sea (pp. 1479, 1528).

In *La casa de Bernarda Alba* speech thus functions as a kind of action
through which power manipulations are demonstrated. Bernarda
structures her world, establishes values and codifies behavior through
language, and it is by linguistic means that the members of her family
accept or reject the ideals of her world. Bernarda's first and final
words in the play—"¡Silencio!"—frame the action, and the strength of
her mandate appears to be identical in both instances. However, upon
close scrutiny it becomes apparent that at the end of the play
Bernarda does not have the same control and forcefulness as she had
at the beginning, nor is her domain as chaste as she would like it to
be. As we have seen, throughout the course of the play attacks are
made from without upon Bernarda's fortress, and resistance to her
supremacy mounts from within: La Poncia recounts the illicit tales of
Paca "la Roseta" and of the young woman who has an illegitimate
child, both of which Bernarda perceives as potentially corruptive
moral influences; Bernarda's daughters begin to reveal their interest
in men, their need for freedom, and their desire to take part in the
activities of the outside world; and the jealousy, rivalry and rebellion
among Bernarda's daughters has produced internal strife and tension.
Furthermore, society, which lurks beyond the walls of Bernarda's
fortress, poses a threat to her omnipotence by virtue of its awareness
of the shame which Adela has brought upon the family.

Changes which occur in Bernarda's speech throughout the course
of the play mirror the effect which these forces have upon her world.
Her language in Act I is characterized by a predominance of directives, in accordance with the fact that at this point Bernarda is in
complete control of her domain. In addition, the tone of Bernarda's
statements is one of confidence and assertiveness, as indicated by the
abundance of exclamations and interrogatives, a potentially aggres-
sive form of speech. After discovering that Angustias has been
watching the men outside her window, for instance, Bernarda becomes furious and attempts to curtail this indecent behavior: "¡Angustias! ¡Angustias!... ¿Qué mirabas y a quién?... ¿Es decente que

---

threatening, [and] vowing." Directives are "illocutionary acts designed to
get the addressee to do something, for example, requesting, commanding,
pleading, inviting, questioning, daring, and insisting or suggesting that
someone do something." (See "Speech Acts and Speech Genres," in *Linguistics for Students of Literature*, p. 229).

una mujer de tu clase vaya con el anzuelo detrás de un hombre el día de la misa de su padre? ¡Contesta! ¿A quién mirabas?... (Avanzando y golpeándola) ¡Suave! ¡Dulzarrona!... ¡Fuera de aquí todas!" (pp. 1454-5). In the second act of the play the number of directives in Bernarda's speech decreases significantly, as she becomes involved in determining the cause of disintegration within her family. It is during this act the La Poncia attempts to transcend her role as servant by voicing authority, which leads to verbal jousting with Bernarda and places the latter on the defensive. It is also during the second act that Bernarda begins to suspect that something dangerous is occurring where Pepe el Romano is concerned. As a result, she begins to listen and respond more to what is being said by the others, rather than instigating conversations and controlling the discussions. During the third and final act of the play, Bernarda continues to be linguistically more reactive than active, as the forces which threaten to undermine her omnipotence close in on her. She must at this point protect the integrity of her household, and, where society is concerned, she must do everything in her power to prevent all outsiders from seeing too much of her world. Noting the extreme importance of the image which her family projects to the outside world, she tells Angustias: "... quiero buena fachada y armonía familiar" (p. 1513). During Act III Bernarda's commands become more softened and the number of directives in her speech continues to be minimal. However, this pattern continues only until the final moments of the play, when Adela hangs herself. With Adela's ultimate rebellion, which causes the fortress walls to dissever and crumble, Bernarda finds herself on the defensive and must do what she can to patch the ever-widening holes in her bastion. Her final words—characterized once more by a predominance of directives-reveal the frantic nature of her struggle to avert defeat and to regain her former position of power and control within a chaste domain:

> ¡Descolgarla! ¡Mi hija ha muerto virgen! Llevadla a su cuarto y vestirla como una doncella. ¡Nadie diga nada! Ella ha muerto virgen... ¡Silencio! ¡A callar he dicho!... Nos hundiremos todas en un mar de luto. Ella, la hija menor de Bernarda Alba, ha muerto virgen. ¿Me habéis oído? ¡Silencio, silencio he dicho! ¡Silencio! (p. 1532).

Bernarda's final words thus leave the spectator with the sense that, despite the image which she wishes to project to the outside world, the house of Bernarda Alba will never be the same. Contact with the exterior has been too extensive to withstand Bernarda's intended insularity, and the view which the outside world has glimpsed of Bernarda's household is not one of purity and perfection. Bernarda Alba's totalitarian regime has met defeat: María Josefa and

Adela have managed to escape the course of inevitability as prescribed by Bernarda and by society, but only through madness and death;[9] La Poncia has demonstrated to Bernarda the fact that she is not afraid to voice her opinions; and Bernarda's daughters have observed not only the outside world but also the models set by Adela, María Josefa and La Poncia. At the end of Lorca's play, the house of Bernarda Alba is merely a shell within which a formerly absolutist ruler struggles to retain control. Bernarda, in turn, is merely the shadow of her former self, as much the victim of social and economic pressure as of her own moral blindness and megalomaniacal tendencies. As a result, the "¡Silencio!" which brings down the final curtain of the play has a hollow ring, and the spectator is left in the midst of a reverberating void. As Eric Bentley has perceptively noted, "With every repetition of the word 'silence' we are more aware of its futility" ("The Poet in Dublin," in In Search of Theater, New York: Vintage Books, 1959, p. 210).

BETHANY COLLEGE

---

[9] It should be noted, as well, that María Josefa speaks in verse throughout the play, an additional means of escaping the prosaic existence prescribed by Bernarda and by society.

Stéfano: Promises and Other Speech Acts

ELISA A. TROIANI

"Mentira. Osté siempre cré a las palabras.
Por eso s'quivoca siempre."
(Discépolo, *Stéfano*, 577)

ROM THE VERY beginning of the play, Discépolo, through Alfonso, calls our attention to language and warns us against his very tools: words can deceive, lead into error or 'equivocation.' Unfortunately, there is no foolproof alternative, since language remains the main means we have to express ourselves. Deeds may later verify or refute what was said, but, until that happens, the hearer must make do with words, however misleading they might be. Furthermore, Alfonso's *mentira* brings up again the long-held contention that all statements are purely descriptive and subject to the True/False test. As this play shows, language has other functions, that speakers consciously or unconsciously exploit, and communication, then, depends on the hearer's ability to understand what the interlocutor is doing.

These issues have long intrigued linguists and philosophers, but it is only with J. L. Austin and his followers, Searle and Grice mainly, that a coherent theory is evolved. As David E. Cooper says in *Philosophy and the Nature of Language*, two of Austin's goals were "to exhibit the variety of acts which can be performed with language" and "to lay down a framework for [their] assessment" (190). Besides, the theory restores to language some of the importance it had lost through an excessive emphasis on psychological interpretation in search of what the writer had really meant. As Stanley E. Fish rightly warns us, in Speech-act theory intention "is a matter of what one takes responsibility for by performing certain conventional (speech) acts. The question of what is going on inside, the question of the '*inward* performance' is simply bypassed" (986).

The application of speech-act theory to *Stéfano* can then help us to meet the open challenge of Alfonso's words, because most utterances are too complex to be rashly dismissed as lies, as he and so many of the other characters in the play do. To achieve true communication the hearer has to go beyond the right/wrong judgement to an understanding of the real function of speech. Besides, Margarita does not err because she believes in words; if she errs it is because she presumes that speakers always assume responsibility for their speech acts. On the other hand, Alfonso errs because he attempts to disregard language itself and focus on the intention behind the words, without realizing that he is instead imposing his own interpretation and bias, thus getting a distorted picture. The application of Speech-act theory, on the contrary, frees critic and reader from the danger of such pseudo-psychological interpretations. Consequently, this paper tries to analyze the play from a linguistic perspective, and see how characters use speech, what consequences their speech acts have, and how such a study may illuminate literary questions like characterization and theme.

The action of *Stéfano* pivots upon a series of promises, made some thirty years before the opening of the play, and the effect of their unfulfillment. Stéfano, young and talented, relying on his ability to make his word true, undertakes a commitment that he is not prepared to meet. The fact is further complicated when, after his initial promise, Stéfano, still on the high wave of illusion and potentiality, keeps making promises which pile up, unfulfilled, finally 'drowning' him (to use Radamés' words) and ruining the whole family. Is Stéfano lying or telling the truth, innocent or guilty, victim or villain?

In "What Is a Speech Act?" John Searle gives us a clue to answer these questions. Searle proposes a set of conditions that promises have to meet to be considered 'sincere' and deals with the questions of insincerity by amending the sincerity condition to read: "S intends that the utterance of T will make him *responsible* for intending to do so" (152). From the dialog in the play, we clearly see that Stéfano's fault is not one of insincerity but of irresponsible use of language. He probably did intend to repay his parents for all they had done for him, to buy his wife diamonds and a house on the Riviera, to write 'la gran ópera.' Accused of bad faith by parents and wife, he finds no excuse. "Papá, tiene razón. No puedo contestarle; no debo contestarle," (589) he admits to Alfonso, and he later accepts Margarita's verdict. "E verdá. E la cruda verdá que me punza el cuore" (599). Stéfano knows that, as Searle's Rule 7 goes, "S intends that the utterance of T will place him under an obligation to do A." This is for Searle "the essential condition" ("What," 150). If the obligation is not seriously taken, the promise is void. Stéfano does not lie or cheat about what he would do, had he succeeded; his mistake is to take intention for fact; to confuse dreams with reality. His hearers, on the other hand, assume that, when he promises, he is undertaking an obligation founded on fact, not chance.

As Stanley Fish says of Coriolanus, "It is his own word that convicts him and it is able to convict him because he has pledged his loyalty to it..." (1000). The difference is, of course, the man behind the promise. Coriolanus, being "complete and sufficient unto himself... a God," (998) assumes full responsibility for his pledge. Stéfano, a twentieth-century anti-hero, wants the world to share his guilt, because he has not only promised to others: he has also promised to himself to be the hero of his own dream. He knows he is indebted to everybody: "Te debo todo lo que te he prometido cuando creía yegar a ser un rey y te ofrecí una corona de oro..." (597); but he also feels he has been a victim of family and society. Alfonso has never understood him and rejects Stéfano's claim "que el dolor del hijo debía saberlo sufrir el padre" (589). The need to feed his family has killed his lyrical strain: "¡Estoy así porque he traído pan a esta mesa día a día!" (586). When he loses his job, he blames "la camorra, la traición" and accuses Pastore of stealing his position. However, it is the failure of his promise to himself which destroys him. The fantastic world he has built around himself proves to be very fragile. Once cracked, it completely collapses. When Stéfano sees the truth— "He visto en un minuto de luche tremenda, tutta la vita mía"—he just gives in: "No existo" (607).

Stéfano's irresponsibility in uttering promises is evident when, after confessing to Margarita the loss of his job with the orchestra, he tries to soothe her saying, "Ma yo te prometo que... Yo te prometo que..." (600). Margarita, who has learned her lesson, refuses to listen. In truth, he can promise nothing at all now; however, the mere act of promising seems to give him some strength.

In her criticism of Speech-act Theory, Michele Rosaldo calls attention to the fact that "the focus of promising in speech-act theory is symptomatic of its commitment to a unified subject" (Quoted in Pratt's "Ideology," 8). This can help us to understand the reason for Stéfano's failure. Stéfano is far from being a unified subject. He fails because he takes upon himself too many commitments: repayment to his parents, richness to his wife, bread to his family, an opera to himself. Furthermore, he is torn in two opposite directions: the world of music, where "todo muriérono a la miseria... por buscarse a sí mismo" (602), and the material world: "Vamo a poder comprar el pópolo" (589) or "yo soñaba cubrire [esta mano] de briyante" (597). As can be expected, he succeeds in neither world. Stéfano confuses personal achievement with material success, and lacks the strength to accept the self-sacrifice and dedication that art demands. Without giving himself a chance to get started in musical creativity, he assumes the economic and moral burden of parents, wife and six children. His talent, if it really existed, gets nipped in the bud by worries over making ends meet and keeping some semblance of peace at home. He sacrifices his music for money, his family for "l'ideale," and finds no satisfaction anywhere.

Rosaldo further remarks that "[M]ore than perhaps any other speech act, promises (when felicitous) confirm the continuity of the individual over time—the beliefs, intentions, abilities and desires that are here today will be there a month or a year from now when the promise falls due" (8-9). That is to say, by promising, Stéfano can exercise some control on the future; consequently, he is, in a sense, living on borrowed time, but, although he can, for a while, delay the time of reckoning when "the promise falls due," this time will inexorably come. Conversely, when promises are not felicitous, the individual is left with a sense of total failure. According to Searle in "A Classification of Illocutionary Acts," promises are commissives whose fit is world to words (12). This means that the person who promises arrogates upon himself the power to make the world match his words; he can create a world by the mere utterance of a few words; he can juggle with reality—a very exhilarating power. When Stéfano can no longer make promises to himself or to others, his life is finished; "Ha pasado. Ha concluido. Ha concluido y no ha empezado" (607).

In his preparatory rule, Searle deals with the other end of the promise: hearers and their expectations. By the act of promising "S intends that the utterance of T will produce in H a belief in words" ("What," 153). If the hearer does not believe that the speaker intends to do as he says, the promise is not valid. Stéfano's tragedy is that he always finds credulous hearers. Alfonso blames María Rosa for the sale of the farm. "Esta póvera fémmena, que ha creído siempre a le parole, yoraba día e noche..." (589). However, he himself had also fallen under the spell of those same words: "E yo, checato, te creí."

Alfonso's words remind us that illocutionary acts like promising may have a perlocutionary effect. They certainly do in *Stéfano*: Alfonso and María Rosa leave their native Italy in search of "la mariposa que nunca s'alcanza" (589); the children "tiéneno que correr, todo rotoso" after the same dream; Margarita marries Stéfano expecting "otra vida, otro ambiente, otro destino..." (599). Pastore and the rest of the orchestra are ready to give up their jobs and make personal sacrifices to help the 'maestro' who will write *the* opera. Alfonso realizes the inherent danger of Stéfano's use of language and warns him: "Nu diche parole. Cayate. Atragátela" (589). Stéfano has built a world of words and, though he himself comes to suspect them, "sigue dichendo parole, yeno d'orgulio" (590).

Misuse of language and disbelief in words are not likely to improve or secure communication. The effect is not only mistrust and alienation, but, also, the destruction of language itself. Mistrust and disappointment have hardened these people, made them selfish and absorbed in themselves, each sheltered in a world of his/her own. Stéfano applies the concept 'world' to Radamés—"¿En qué mundo vive Ud., hijo?" (592)—and to himself: "Ése es su mundo... Yo pienso en el mío" (614). They have all become like the oyster in Stéfano's metaphor: "L'alegría, el dolor, la fiesta, el yanto, lo gritos, la música ajena, no la inquietan. Se caya solitaria. La preocupa solamente lo que precisa, lo que tiene adentro, su ritmo" (585). Ironically, Stéfano wishes "¡Quí fuera ostra!" without realizing that he also shares "su silencio," which he calls "un talento." Stéfano does not understand that this kind of silence and self-absorption is negative for the artist, whose resources are 'l'alegría, el dolor, etc.' It is also detrimental to him as a human being, since it breeds egoism, indifference, ingratitude.

Discépolo extends the social validity of this concept through the use of Radamés, whom Dowling labels "el portavoz de la conciencia moral colectiva" ("Stéfano," 60). Radamés, Stéfano's sixteen-year-old son, lives in a world of his own. He trusts language and believes in its power "to bring about the correspondence between the propositional context and reality." His kind of speech acts is declaratives (Searle, "Classification," 13). "¿Usted me puso este nombre, papá? Está mal. Yo me debía llamar Salvador," he reproaches Stéfano (591). His dream is to be a savior, but, unlike his operatic namesake, he is not interested in glory. People's indifference—even if in a dream—angers him. "La gente abajo aplaudía. Sería mejor que en vez de aplaudir la gente ayudase" (591). Radamés is further puzzled when in another dream, after he has saved all the victims of a shipwreck, "se fueron todos corriendo sin darse vuelta" (614). Stéfano tries to comfort him. "Mejor. No hay que cobrar los favores," but Radamés is still at a loss. "Yo me senté a pensar, pensar." Radamés is the only one aware of the need to love and help each other: "... la gente... se quema porque uno no oye que gritan socorro, socorro" (579). He does not realize, however, that his own family is drowning and burning.

While Stéfano depends on commissives to escape reality, Radamés depends on declaratives. He cannot distinguish between tenor and vehicle. He fails to keep dreams, day-dreams and nightmares, separate from reality. In the end he does not know if he is awake or asleep. The world around him has become as chaotic and frightening as his nightmares. Both, father and son, blur the line between reality and dreams. As Stéfano fails to fulfill promises founded on fancy, Radamés' words and dreams fail to become reality. If he is not 'Radamés' in real life, he is 'Salvador' only in dreams. His awareness of human misery and failings is vague and general. Stéfano dies alone. All Radamés impatiently notices is that the light is still on.

Alfonso's speech acts are of two kinds: directives, with little or no perlocutionary effect, addressed to María Rosa generally and Stéfano sometimes, and constatives or representatives, whose point is to commit the speaker to the truth of an expressed proposition, and their fit words to world (Searle, "Classification," 12). However, as Cooper argues, "a constative utterance is liable to just as many types of infelicities as performatives. Just as I can promise insincerely, I can report insincerely" (194). This distinction is important to us because, while Discépolo uses Alfonso to provide most of the background information, at the same time he drops enough hints to remind us that, as reporter and interpreter, Alfonso is both limited and biased.[1]

Besides, Alfonso is unable to establish links. For Dowling he is "el ejemplo por excelencia de la ostra" (58). He refuses to conform to the new family and country, as shown by his language, the most 'italianized' of all. Still tied to "la terra co la viña, la oliva e la pumarola," he has lost the bases for his existence, "Tierra, familia e religione," (587) and rejects Margarita and her children, products of another world. He also rejects Stéfano, and flatly admits, "Yo no t'ho comprendido nunca" (585). When, softened by his "cañita," he tries to make contact with his son, he fails ludicrously. "¿Qué tiene? ¿Te duélono la muela? Por eso no come hace tanto día" (600). His world is eons apart from Stéfano's, who, from his perspective, sees "(Por el padre) [U]n campesino iñorante que pegado a la tierra no ve ni siente; (por el mismo) un iluso que ve y siente" (619). Far from the land, Alfonso has become a grotesque old man, acting sometimes like a child, sometimes like a tyrant, always like a victim.

As shown in the minidrama that opens the play, Alfonso's relation to María Rosa is ambiguous. He resents her moaning and blames her for all their misfortunes, but needs her as somebody over whom to assert his authority. Cowed by Margarita, disregarded by his grandchildren, only María Rosa sees in him those qualities and attitudes he equates with manliness ('enojado,' 'terco,' 'que forza tiene,' 'un diablo'). She maintains for him an appearance of authority, shielding him from the truth,[2] or reminding Radamés, "tenga rispeto"

---

[1] The same applies to Stéfano's constatives, as in his long conversation with Pastore.

[2] Notice this exchange:

M   ... En víctima, no. No las puedo soportar.
    A   (*Tartamedeando de ira*) ¿A quí? ¿A... nosotro?
M. R.   (*apresurada*) No; a las víctimas.
    A   Ah.

(579). He pretends to need María Rosa's mediation to understand what is said, hides behind the mask of incomprehension. However, he understands more than he pretends to and can manipulate language to fit his aims. In directives Alfonso finds some of the power and manliness he has lost in Stéfano's house. Constatives allow him to gloss over reality and evade his share of responsibility. If reality does not suit the role he wants to play, he can twist words and try to force events, as he does in the Epilog.

Esteban's handling of language is different: he uses a great many directives trying to get Margarita off his neck. Besides, many of his constatives also have a clear directive point. "Me atormenta saber que usted me aguarda," or "[E]s amor mal entendido pesar sobre quien se quiere" (582) are true entreaties to Margarita, who clearly understands their point and rejects them with a 'No' which, otherwise, would be quite inappropriate, since she is not denying the truth of a regular representative but refusing to accept Esteban's indirect use of language to persuade her.

Esteban does not have much to say, and when he does speak, he falls into ready-made phrases with low semantic value which simple souls associate with poetry. "Está triste la calle. Es un verso" (610). Appropriately, his room is 'un altillo' (the working class equivalent of the ivory tower), and he keeps aloof. Stéfano's crisis shakes him out of this pose. His first attempt to bridge the gap with his father, from a pseudo-intellectual, pseudo-poetic stand, fails because Esteban can only repeat clichés that Stéfano himself has used with no success. When he is gripped by anguish, empty phrases give way to simple words. "Papá... Figlio..." The barrier between them falls and, with it, Esteban's blinders. As the stage direction informs us, "Esteban... mira [a la familia] como si los viese por primera vez" (620). Furthermore, poetry, which has so far been elusive, rewards him with "un verso bello." "Todo ese dolor por un verso. ¿Vale tan poco la vida?" wonders Stéfano (621). However, Esteban has gained more than a poem; he has recovered language itself: he can express his true self, stop repeating high-flown formulas.

All characters in Stéfano are adroit users of clichés and sententious statements. "Hijo chico, dolore chico; hijo grande, dolore grande," recites María Rosa (583). "Soy feliz cumpliendo" insists Esteban (582); "... la vita es una cosa molesta que te ponen a la espalda cuando nace e hay que seguir sosteniendo aunque te pese," philosophizes Stéfano (587). "Casi siempre lo que no se comprende hoy es la luz de mañana," he explains to Ñeca (595); "La vida es como uno quiere que sea" says Esteban (619). The list is long; this sample is enough as an illustration of their use.

In "Toward a Rhetoric of the Stage," Ruth Amossy discusses several definitions of clichés. Her conclusion: "a rhetorical figure [which] turns from overuse into a fixed formula, and is therefore perceived by the reader as a 'trite expression'" (52). The cliché has a twofold beauty for the speaker: it exudes credibility; it allows him/her to shirk responsibility. As an anonymous utterance accepted in the language through years of usage, clichés carry a weight which is independent of their True/False value. Being difficult to refute, they become very useful when speakers are on the losing side of an argument. An example: on hearing of Stéfano's loss of his job, Margarita blames him for all their sufferings; Stéfano only answers in clichés to stay her flow of reproaches. Through clichés, responsibility, guilt, blame, can be evaded for a while. However, when their hollowness becomes apparent, when reality is seen without colored lenses, the result is chaos. "Ésta es una mirada que degrada, que reduce y destruye toda dignidad y solemnidad con que esos valores siempre fueron investidos" (Kaiser-Lenoir, 170). In the Epilog, when Stéfano takes a cynical look around the room, the long respected clichés fall shattered, to be replaced by the crudest realism. Thus, "l'amor de la mujer," which tranditonally is "l'único premio del hombre," suddenly is seen as "¡estúpido sensualismo!" (616-17). His family, as in Radamés' nightmare, have become "todo bicho y animale" (620). Obviously, clichés do little to improve the quality of communication. They alienate and conceal rather than link and reveal.

Another powerful barrier is the variety of languages used. It is possible, in *Stéfano*, to speak of femenine and masculine idiolects. The women in this play, true products of this conservative society of the Thirties, have no lives of their own, orbit around their men. Thus, Margarita, repeating María Rosa's mistake, has centered her hopes on her son Esteban. Ñeca, an eighteen-year-old who behaves like a child, only thinks of Stéfano's happiness, feels responsible for him. María Rosa, neglected by her son, has become Alfonso's mother, protecting him and stealing a few cents for his 'cañita'. The three are mother figures; their worlds are made of feelings, not ideas. They do not understand, but can truly love; as María Rosa says, "Te quiero... e ya está" (591). As long as this is enough for them, they can give their men peace and quiet. "... si yo hubiera nacido nada má que para tenerla así... yorando por lo que yoro... yo, estaría bien pago de haber nacido," explains Stéfano to an uncomprehending weeping Ñeca. (595). This peace, however, is brief.

The three women express themselves mainly through tears, moans, complaints ("Pobre papá." "Pobre m'hijito.") or clichés. María Rosa insists on clarity of meaning. She translates, and often 'interprets', for her husband. Alfonso, impatient, uses language loosely, often maliciously downgrading his topic, as when he calls the conservatory of music a school or speaks of Stéfano "sonando el trombone a una banda" (590). María Rosa is always quick to correct him. In general, the play shows men handling language more freely, women more timidly, even when uttering clichés. "Todo lo que se resiste vale," pontificates Margarita, but when Esteban wants to know, "¿Cómo lo sabe?" she, unsure, asks, "¿Está mal?" (610-11). Confined to a secondary role and a situation of dependence, women often use language ingratiatingly, to gain sympathy, love, attention. "¡Qué lindo mi hijo!... Tan bueno; tan consciente... Tan serio; tan hombre," says Margarita to her embarrassed son (582). María Rosa flirts with Alfonso and pretends to be a helpless old woman to secure his company for a short while (577-80).

Each member of the family also has his/her own lexical variety. Most important are Esteban's, with emphasis on pseudo-poetic expressions, and Stéfano's, a transliteration of feelings and sensations into musical phrases. This jargon seems to give him a vantage-point and a shield from which he can both defend himself and attack others. As defence, we see him respond to Alfonso's "La vita no e solo pane; la vita e tambiene pache e contento" with the irrelevant "Entonces... alegrémono, papá... A este 'andante brioso', pongámoe un ... 'allegro'... un 'allegro' ma 'non troppo'" (586). Devoid of reasonable arguments to convince him, Stéfano hides behind words Alfonso is in no position to contest. His attack on Pastore through the common language of music is even more cruel, because it is directed at shaming him in his professional pride: "Tú terminas tocando la corneta al soterráneo" (605).

There are also different dialects in use. Alfonso uses 'cocoliche'; Margarita and Esteban 'rioplatense'; Radamés and Ñeca's 'agüelo/a' point to a suburban or countrified dialect; Stéfano, María Rosa, and Pastore, move between 'cocoliche' and Argentinian. The clash of dialects provides some of the comicity of the play; it is also one of the devices Discépolo employs to foreground language. (Another is María Rosa's insistence on correctness.) Two instances are interesting: when Alfonso says 'frigorífico' for 'jeroglífico' (585) and when Stéfano hesitates between 'mazamorra' and 'mazmorra' (613). In the first case, the slip of the tongue directs out attention to the lack of love between father and son, and anticipates Stéfano calling his own son "la fría cassatta" (616). In the second case, the house has become not only a dungeon but also a thick porridge in which Stéfano drowns. The interpretation is not far-fetched. When Stéfano is lying on the floor, with a foot stuck on the leg of the table, he whispers, "Uh... cuanta salsa... Cómo sube..." (621).

The result of all this linguistic variety is poor communication, even between father and son. When Alfonso says he has never believed in him, Stéfano answers, "En eso sabía más que yo. Conocía la madera." Alfonso, the immigrant who never adjusted, asks María Rosa, "¿Qué matera?" (590). Other times, the semantic meaning of words is clear, but force and referent are misrepresented or supplemented with personal intentions. (See 620-21). Furthermore, characters fail to distinguish between ironic and sincere speech, or choose to understand what re-inforces their beliefs—not what is being said.[3]

For J. L. Austin, illocutionary acts of the kind exhibited in this play have to achieve a certain effect to be considered successful.[4] This effect "amounts to bringing about the understanding of *the meaning* and of *the force* of the locution" (my italics). He calls this requirement "the securing of uptake." Not only are illocutionary acts "bound up with effects," but they also invite a response (117). In the world of *Stéfano*, none of this happens. Trying to exploit language to serve their own purposes, the characters have simply destroyed it. The mechanism and the pieces are still there, but they do not click together any more. People have even ceased to listen to each other, only hear their own voices, as illustrated in this exchange:

> STEFANO ... ¡Uno debería despedazarse para hacerle a cada uno un paraíso de esta tierra infernale! Y en cambio...
>
> MARGARITA (sentada a la mesa) Y en cambio...
>
> STEFANO (La había olvidado; la mira con una ceja alta.) En cambio... (Se pone a trabajar...) (595).

Seemingly there is one signified, but context and stage directions show each of them absorbed in his/her own thoughts.

Radamés and Stéfano seem to be able to communicate in a make-believe world where Stéfano has composed "una gran ópera" which,

---

[3] Notice this conversation between Stéfano and his father:
    A E yo sé perqué m'engañaste: de haragane. No te gustaba zapá.
    S ¡Verdad sacrosanta!
    A ¿Ha visto?
Here Alfonso choses not to notice the irony, which runs counter to his argument. A few lines below, however, exactly the opposite occurs.
    S (con seria convicción) Sí, saría mejor enseñarle a correr lo chancho.
    A Se burla.

[4] There are three kinds of speech acts: locutionary (the phonetic and syntactical constructs); illocutionary, "the basic unit of linguistic communication" according to Searle in "Classification (2), or, as Cooper puts it, "the act, like promising, which we perform in uttering certain words in context" (193); and prelocutionary, or "what is performed *by* uttering certain words."

Radamés assures, "yo oí. La tocaron al teatro" (614). Outside the
realm of fantasy, however, their conversation sometimes fails.

> RADAMES ¿No es tarde, papá?
> STEFANO Sí... muy tarde.
> RADAMES Vaya a dormir, entonce. (Se enrosca.)
> STEFANO (Sonríe) Uh... No se apure tanto... Pronto voy a ir
> (614).

A simple conversation, on the surface exhibiting 'coherence and
continuity', on close analysis shows the abysmal gap between the
speakers. Radamés is calling attention to how late it is; he is tired and
wants to go back to sleep. For Stéfano, on the other hand, the
question refers back to his just announced liberation: "yo también me
he liberado de todo lo dolore ajeno. Ahora pienso para mí solo" (614).
When he agrees, then, he admits that his determination has come too
late, since his talent is now wasted. Continuing with his own train of
thought, Radamés responds to this 'Sí' with a suggestion that his
father should go to bed. Stéfano, who has premonitions of his death,
asks Radamés to be patient. He will go (die) soon enough.

How can these two readings co-exist? How is conversation
possible when both speakers have different referents in mind? How
do readers / audience detect the meaning of Stéfano's replies? As Grice
reminds us, every talk exchange takes place on two levels of
communication: what is said and what is implied (or implicated). He
speaks of Conventional Implicature, when conventional meaning
determines what is said and implicated, and Non-Conventional
Implicature, when what is implied is other than what is said (25). In
this short exchange, two things happen simultaneously: Radamés and
Stéfano conduct their conversation on one level (Conventional
Implicature), therefore getting one sense of each other's words and
responding accordingly. The reader / audience's uptake is on a
different level (Non-Conventional Implicature), where context,
authorial directions, and acting provide the clues which modify what
is *said* and bring out what is *implied*.

Questions are another linguistic tool characters often use to
perform a variety of functions. "¿Está aquí?" asks María Rosa to
pretend that she has not heard Alfonso arrive (576). Margarita will
later use the same words to express her anger at Stéfano (593).
Often, questions are shy, reticent ways of expressing affection, care.
"¿Te vas ya?... ¿No querés otro mate?... ¿Llevás pañuelo?" (582)
serve Margarita to show her feelings for Esteban and to detain him a
little longer. Other times, questions are meant to corner people and
reduce them to silence. When confronted by Alfonso, Stéfano
counterattacks: "¿Falta el pane aquí? ¿Ha faltado alguna vez el pane?"

(586). The hearer has no option. 'Yes' would mean they had gone hungry—apparently untrue. 'No' would amount to saying that all is well. As Alfonso realizes, the only possibility is to comment on the question: "La vita no e solo pane."

Sometimes through questions the character can better understand or absorb what he/she is being told. "¿El puesto?... ¿El puesto en la orquesta?... ¿Ya no tenés el puesto?... ¿Después de diez años?" (597) is Margarita's tirade when Stéfano announces he has been fired. None of these questions need an answer: Margarita is only trying to absorb a piece of news that will have a shattering effect on their lives. It is important to notice the punctuation here, the pauses between the questions, as if Margarita could hear herself silently answering.

Questions can also express an attitude. Margarita, again, provides us with an excellent example. "Ah, ¿estás aquí? ¿Querés comer? La Ñeca está llorando en la cocina porque no cenaste. ¿Qué mirás? ¿Terminaste la partiture? ¿Qué mirás?" (593). Only the iterated question gets an indirect answer when Stéfano tells her to pick up her stockings. She takes this as a negative answer to her second question and concludes, "¿No querés comer, entonces?" and immediately after voices her complaint: "Todo para hacerme sufrir." If we attend to the context, we see that only the question '¿qué mirás?' is a real interrogative. The first utterance "Ah, ¿estás aquí?" in isolation, could mean several things: surprise, joy, plain verification, or, as here, regret and anger. Discépolo does not give precise instructions on the intonation to use, but the stage directions preceding this speech clearly set the atmosphere: "Entra Margarita. Nada tiene que hacer... pero mueve las sillas, sacude, arregla." The useless activities she undertakes show the audience the mounting tension within Margarita and anticipate her snappy remark. Punctuation helps the reader, loading the stage directions with unstated meaning. Furthermore, we notice that Margarita does not care whether Stéfano wants to eat or not. She does not press the issue and jumps to her conclusion. The question on the 'partitura' is a poor attempt to call Stéfano's attention away from her.

Margarita leaves after this brief exchange. Obviously, she only wanted to express her antagonism and frustration, not to get responses from Stéfano. A similar case occurs later when Stéfano verbally attacks Pastore. In these instances communication fails because the speaker is not interested in dialog. The hearer may understand this and, like Stéfano, remain silent, or he may naively take the questions at face value and try to answer, like Pastore. He will soon realize, though, that here no answer can be correct, since all his interlocutor wants is a springboard from which to launch a verbal attack.

Commands and threats are also frequent throughout the play. Some of them are void becaue their conditions are not properly met, as when Alfonso says "¡Va! ¡Va!" and the stage direction adds, "Echando al nieto que se ha ido" (579). Most often, commands and threats are totally ignored, either because the hearer is 'caprichioso', like Alfonso; or impatient, like Ofelia, Aníbal and Atilio; or because the hearer does not grant the speaker the higher status or position which is needed for this illocutionary act to be felicitously performed. Therefore, commands and threats carry no meaning, have become empty forms used out of habit. This points not only to the collapse of communication but also to the collapse of moral authority.

What the plays shows us, then, is a gradual loss of communicative skills and the ensuing distrust and fear of words which make characters even refuse to hear what others have to say. When Stéfano cannot stop Margarita from talking about their dead son Santiaguito, he drops a stone to startle her out of her reverie (506). Likewise, when Stéfano starts rhapsodizing about humanity— "Este espectáculo de la perversidad humana me llena de tristeza"— Margarita brings him back to her level of reality by asking "¿No le vas a romper la cara?" (598). Because she has learnt to distrust language, however, she can quickly detect the truth hidden behind evasive, florid words. "Algo ha ocurrido. Me vas a dar una mala noticia," is her response to Stéfano's halting apologies (597).

This gradual loss of communicative power is, naturally, best exemplified in Stéfano. As a man, Stéfano has lost the ability to express his ideas. This loss of linguistic competence is the sequel of his loss of musical ability: from 'medalla d'oro' of that Naples conservatory, "direttore a un teatro," and composer of "l'ópera fenomenale' to "la cabra," whose instrument cannot be heard; to a mere copier of other people's music, which has destroyed his own. "El canto se ha perdido... Lo ajeno ha aplastado lo mío" (607). He loses both abilities: to create and to perform. "Lo músico de orquestra, hijo, so casi siempre artistas fracasados que se han hecho obreros" (592). Radamés quickly understands: "Como a la fábrica... Es un baruyo, pero le pagan." It is the prostitution of art: music performed for a price; music as an object. "Usted va a *fabricar* una gran ópera" (my italics). The orchestra is no longer a harmonious company of artists but a cacophonous group of individuals, each making his own noise. Communication fails in both of Stéfano's worlds: orchestra and home; music and words.

In the Epilog, Stéfano's further deterioration is shown in his total loss of musical and linguistic competence. Drunk, he can only sing a monotonous nursery rhyme to an audience of lamps, tables and chairs. Freed from restraints, he can finally do what he has always wanted: snap the chains that have bound him. In the same way he breaks all he finds in his way with his old overcoat, he cuts off the links that tied him to his family with direct insult and cruel irony. He replaces the trombone—his instrument in the orchestra—for an imaginary mandolina—associated with songs of love and joy—to upturn through mockery all those myths that keep a family together. What follows is pandemonium: the women are reduced to moans and tears, Alfonso to silence; only Esteban can still repeat his hope-sustaining clichés. Radamés, an unwilling spectator, decides: "Sigo soñando. Es una pesadiya" (620). Language, stretched to breaking-point throughout the play, has finally snapped. Underneath the deceiving words with which they have tried to comfort themselves lurks a reality that will finally prevail.

A linguistic analysis of the play yields many clues on which to base a study of the characters and themes of the play. It even partly justifies the emphasis on socio-political criticism the play has usually received, and whose main thrust is to present Stéfano as victim to the Conservative Argentine government of the Thirties.[5] Argentina, confident in her resources and posibilities, lures European immigration with the promise of personal fulfilment and economic success. A textual reading of the play will allow this political extension only as the projection of the microcosm inhabited by Stéfano and his family. Thus projected, Stéfano will become an allegorial representation of that institution which has supposedly victimized him. Both have made the same mistakes: they have promised irresponsibly, confused the spiritual with the economic, failed to make their promises true. They have rejected reality and replaced it for clichés and myths devoid of meaning. As Kaiser-Lenoir points out, Stéfano's family has to live on the myths Stéfano created for himself (73). By extension, we can say that society has to accept the political slogans and make them its own. As in *Stéfano*, when myths become suspect, when language itself becomes suspect, the result is chaos and alienation. The macrocosm can be Argentina in the Thirties, or can be any place, and any time, wherever and whenever language is falsified and acts, at daggers with words, fail to be genuine speech-acts.

COLLEGE OF SAINT SCHOLASTICA

---

[5] See Claudia Kaiser-Lenoir and David Viñas, for example.

Works Cited

Amossy, Ruth. "Toward a Rhetoric of the Stage: The Scenic Realization of Verbal Clichés." *Poetics Today,* 2.3 (1981): 49-63

Austin, J. L. *How to Do Things with Words.* New York: Oxford University Press, 1962.

Cooper, David E. "Speech Acts." *Philosophy and the Nature of Language.* London: Longman, 1973.

Discépolo, Armando. *Obras escogidas.* Tomo 3. Buenos Aires: Editorial Álvarez, 1969.

Dowling, Lee H. "El problema de comunicación en *Stéfano* de Armando Discépolo." *LATR* 13:2 (Spring 1968): 57-63.

Elam, Keir. *The Semiotics of Theater and Drama.* London: Methuen, 1980.

Fish, Stanley E. "How to Do Things with Austin and Searle: Speech Act Theory and Literary Criticism." *MLN* 91 (1976): 983-1025.

Grice, H. Paul. "Logic and Conversation." Cole and Morgan (eds.) *Syntax and Semantics.* Vol. III: Speech Acts, 1975.

Hancher, Michael. "Beyond a Speech-Act Theory of Literary Discourse." *MLN* 92 (1977): 1079-98.

Kayser-Lenoir, Claudia. *El grotesco criollo: estilo teatral de una época.* La Habana: Casa de las Américas, 1977.

Ohmann, Richard. "Speech Acts and the Definition of Literature" *Philosophy and Rhetoric,* 4 (Winter, 1971): 1-19.

——————. "Speech, Action and Style." *Literary Style: A Symposium.* Oxford University Press, 1971.

——————. "Speech, Literature, and the Space Between." *NLH* 4 (1972): 47-63.

Ordaz, Luis. "Sesenta años de dramaturgia rectora: el teatro de Armando Discépolo." Armando Discépolo, *Giácomo, Babilonia, Cremona.* Buenos Aires: Editorial Talía, 1970.

Pratt, Mary Louise. *Toward a Speech Act Theory of Literary Discourse.* Bloomington: Indiana University Press, 1977.

——————. "The Ideology of Speech Act Theory." *Centrum* 1:1 (Spring 1981): 5-18.

——————. and Elizabeth Closs Traugott. "Speech Acts and Speech Genres." *Linguistics for Students of Literature.* New York: Harcourt, Brace, Jovanovich, 1980.

Searle, John R. "What is a Speech Act?" In *Language and Social Context: Selected Readings.* Ed. Pier Paolo Giglioli. Harmondsworth: Penguin Education, 1976, 136-54.

——————. "A Classification of Illocutionary Acts." *Language in Society,* 5 (1976): 1-23.

Seung, T. K. "Pragmatic Norms," in *Semiotics and Thematics in Hermeneutics.* New York: Columbia University Press, 1982.

Viñas, David. "Grotesco, inmigración y fracaso." In Armando Discépolo, *Obras escogidas,* Tomo I. Buenos Aires: Editorial Álvarez, 1969, VII-LXIII.

Reversals of Illocutionary Logic
in Griselda Gambaro's
Las paredes

ROBERT A. PARSONS

LTHOUGH GRISELDA GAMBARO is now widely recognized as one of Spanish America's most important and original contemporary playwrites, critics have only recently begun to examine her individual works. Her best-known dramas are *Las paredes* (1963), *El desatino* (1965), *Los siameses* (1967), and *El campo* (1967). A common theme in these plays, many of which have been staged both in her native Argentina and abroad, is the dehumanization of average men and women by repressive social and political forces.

This study is concerned with Gambaro's first play *Las paredes*, a powerful and moving drama for which she was awarded first prize in the 1963 competition of the Asociación Santafecina de Teatros Independientes (Holzapfel, 5). Although it displays many of the techniques of dramatic expression that surface in Gambaro's later works, *Las paredes* has been the object of very little critical attention. Some of the early overviews of Gambaro's work, such as Carballido's, do not mention *Las paredes* at all. Dauster also makes no reference to *Las paredes* in his note on the evolution of Gambaro's drama from "absurdist forms to a seemingly more realistic form" (56). And Holzapfel excludes *Las paredes* from her discussion of the relationship of Gambaro's drama to the Theatre of the Absurd, concentrating on what she calls "the author's most significant works," *El desatino*, *Los siameses*, and *El campo* (5).

Cypess, on the other hand, devotes several pages to a general discussion of plot, theme, and dramatic technique in *Las paredes*, which she considers one of Gambaro's four major plays ("The Plays," 95). In another article, Cypess discusses briefly the relationship of the changing physical environment to character transformation in *Las paredes* ("Physical Imagery," 358). The need for general discussion of the characteristics of Gambaro's plays has diminished with the growth of her reputation and the increased accessibility of her works. The focus of recent studies by Foster, Gerdes, Picón Garfield, and Postma, has shifted to analysis of individual works. The only detailed study of *Las paredes* published to date, however, is that of Peter L. Podol, who further develops ideas suggested by Cypess in "Physical Imagery." Podol compares *Las paredes* to Buero Vallejo's *La fundación*, noting the presence in both plays of "a dramatic milieu permeated with imprisoning totalitarian forces" and "the need on the part of the protagonists to seek refuge in a subjective, inner reality" (44). The focus of Podol's study is upon Gambaro's and Buero's use of metamorphosing stage settings to alter both the audience's and characters' perception of reality.

The one component of Gambaro's plays that has been consistently neglected in both the early and the more recent critical studies is language. A number of critics have called attention to Gambaro's extensive use of Artaudian techniques that stress the communicative power of gesture, facial expression, lighting effects, and a variety of human and non-human sounds designed to surprise or shock the audience (Holazpfel, 5-6; Cypess, "The Plays," 95; Gerdes, 11). Cypess goes so far as to claim that "dialogue can be considered of secondary importance" in Gambaro's theater ("The Plays," 95). This may appear to be so because Gambaro's characters use short sentences, non-rhetorical language, and uncomplicated grammatical structures. Precisely these qualities, however, make language an efficient instrument of coercion. Moreover, although it is terse and laconic, the language of the dialogue is often deceptively complex and highly ambiguous within the specific contexts of Gambaro's plays.

The relationship between dialogue and theatrical effects in Gambaro's plays is both contradictory and complementary. In *Las paredes*, for example, the frequent incongruity between sounds, gestures, and movements, on the one hand, and the sense of the dialogue, on the other, serves to enhance rather than diminish the power of language. This is because the contradictory relationship between dialogue and theatrical effects reinforces the contradictory logic within the dialogue itself. The purpose of this study is to identify and analyze the verbal strategies used by two characters in *Las paredes*, the Funcionario and the Ujier, to oppress and manipulate the behavior of the third character, the Joven. Although some commentary on the ambiguous interplay of theatrical effects and dialogue is essential, a detailed consideration of this complex relationship is beyond the scope of the paper.

This analysis draws on the theory of speech acts developed by J. L. Austin in *How To Do Things with Words* and refined by John Searle and other theorists. Austin's central idea is that in uttering certain types of sentences, one in fact performs an action. Thus, if I say "I'll take the blue one" under the proper circumstances, for example, while trying to decide on the right sweater in the presence of a sales clerk, I will have made a purchase. Austin called such utterances, which in theory include all sentences, illocutionary acts. His initial attempt to classify illocutionary acts proved problematical, but Searle has since identified five general classes of illocutionary acts, which can be summarized as follows:

REPRESENTA-
TIVES: Speaker posits existence of a certain proposition or state of affairs. Examples: descriptions, statements, predictions.

DIRECTIVES: Speaker attempts to affect the future behavior of hearer. Examples: challenges, commands, requests.

COMMISSIVES: Speaker commits him/herself to a future course of action. Examples: promises, declarations of support, guarantees.

EXPRESSIVES: Speaker expresses his/her own psychological state. Examples: welcomes, expressions of condolence or sympathy, congratulations.

DECLARATIONS: Speaker's words create new state of affairs. Examples: firing, christening, sentencing, decreeing. ("Classification," 10-16)[1]

In speech-act theory human discourse is regarded as an extended exchange of different types of illocutionary acts governed by pragmatic rules of social convention. Each utterance carries an illocutionary force that is context-dependent. A statement such as "It's hot in here" falls into the category of representatives by the criteria of grammatical structure and literal meaning. Under certain circumstances, however, it can be both intended and understood as a request or order (directives) to turn on the air conditioning, open the window, or move the party outside. Normal conversation, then, involves a constant effort on the part of both speaker and hearer, whose roles are inverted with every speech exchange, to determine the illocutionary force or implied meaning of each utterance.

---

[1] Elam (166-167) provides an excellent summary of Searle's categories with examples of illocutionary utterances of each type from Shakespearian plays. Hancher (13) has revised Searle's classification to take into account an important hybrid class of illocutionary acts that he calls "commissive-directives."

In theater, such non-verbal effects as off-stage sounds, facial expressions, intonation, and movements function generally as "illocutionary force indicators" of dramatic dialogue (Elam, 166). In Gambaro's works, however, these devices are often at odds with the dialogue, so that rather than clarifying the illocutionary force of an utterance, as is their normal function, they frequently create ambiguity.[2]

The analysis of dialogic discourse, whether in fictional or real-life contexts, involves other factors as well. Mary Louise Pratt faults speech-act theorists for their failure to take into account, among other things, the power relations that exist between participants in a speech exchange. Noting that speech roles are often not a matter of choice, she points out that it is "common for one person or group to be defining the purpose of an encounter, determining what quantity is enough, what topics are relevant, what counts as truth and adequate evidence, who gets to speak at all" ("Ideology," 13).

The course and outcome of all speech exchanges in *Las paredes* are determined by the power relationship that prevails among the three characters, the Funcionario, the Ujier, and the Joven. From the opening scenes the Joven's subordinate position in the hierarchy of power is apparent. The setting is a room, diminishing in size as the play progresses, where the Joven is being held for reasons that are never specified. The Funcionario and the Ujier, who control the Joven's physical circumstance, his freedom of movement, conspire to gain control of his mind as well.

The action consists of a series of conversations between the Joven and his tormentors. The Joven is primarily concerned with the reason and length of his detention. Although the Funcionario's and the Ujier's power is absolute from the outset, they use devious and cruel forms of verbal manipulation to raise and shatter alternatively the Joven's hopes for release. Their apparent motive for prolonging the Joven's uncertainty is to get him to consent to his own victimization and ultimate destruction.

Some of the more obvious strategies the Funcionario and the Ujier use require little explanation. These include accusing the Joven of twisting and changing the meaning of their words; the excessive use of politeness formulas and ironic displays of false concern for the Joven's well being; and the use of insinuation and ominous references to the Joven's death or other terrible fates.

The more complex verbal tactics fall into two broad categories: 1) the use of contradictory illocutionary logic, and 2) the subversion of language's communicative capacity through the negation of the referential value of words, the truth value of representative

---

[2] See Savona for an illuminating study of stage directions as speech acts.

illocutionary utterances, and the obligatory value of commissive illocutionary utterances. The rest of this study is an analysis of each of these categories.

The contradictory logic of the first category is apparent in the semantical contradictions at the sentence level of the Funcionario's and the Ujier's speech. When the Funcionario assures the Joven, for example, that the detainees are "dueños absolutos de nuestra habitación" (20), the first-person plural possessive pronoun that qualifies *habitación* contradicts the idea of absolute ownership expressed at the beginning of the statement. On another occasion, the Ujier extorts all the Joven's money as well as his billfold in exchange for some "novedades viejas" about his fate. The Ujier says he came into possession of this coveted imformation "casualmente, pegando el oído a la puerta" (55).

The contradictory logic at the semantic level within sentences is paralleled at the pragmatic level of dialogic exchange. Again, visual effects often mirror or enhance the impact of logical inconsistencies in the dialogue. The appearance in the opening scene of the Ujier, whose "barba... despareja y de varios días" contrasts with "el aseo del uniforme" (9), foreshadows the contradictions of the dialogue that follows (Podol, 45). Reacting to a sudden cry for help that breaks a prolonged silence and then fades away into a suffocated scream, the Joven jumps to his feet:

> JOVEN ¿Escuchó?
> UJIER (*natural*) Sí, sí.
> JOVEN ¿Qué ha sido?
> UJIER Un grito. (*Sonriendo*) Alguien a quien se le cayó la pared encima.
> JOVEN Alguien gritaba pidiendo socorro.
> UJIER ¿Sí? No crea. La acústica. Defecto de construcción, ladrillos mal cocidos. Negligencia. Es borchornoso, pero no se puede tirar la casa abajo, por eso.
> JOVEN Era una persona, una voz.
> UJIER (*admirado*) ¿De quién?
> JOVEN De alguien. No sé.
> UJIER (*paternal*) Sueña. (*Se rasga una oreja*) ¿Escuchó?
> JOVEN (*atiende, luego*) No. Ahora no.
> UJIER ¡Cómo lo engañan sus sentidos! Me rasqué una oreja y cuando lo hago, la tormpeta de Eustaquio suena como una orquesta. ¡Bom! ¡Bom! Costumbre.
> JOVEN Pero antes, antes "sí" escuché un grito, una llamada de auxilio. Parecía alguien... a punto de entregar su alma.

UJIER (*divertido*) ¡Nunca lo hubiera expresado así! Decimos liquidado, muerto. Incluso fenecido. Pero "Entregar su alma"..., es hermoso, poético. ¿Es usted escritor?
JOVEN No.
UJIER Es una lástima. Tiene condiciones (9-10).

At the beginning of the exchange the Ujier responds to the Joven's requests for verification and clarification of the scream with an unequivocal affirmation and a seemingly absurd explanation offered with a smile and an indifferent tone that contrast markedly with the apparent urgency of the situation. The Ujier then turns aside the Joven's attempt to clarify further the situation with an obscure explanation about acoustics and faulty masonry. The Joven responds with a reaffirmation of the scream's reality. The Ujier counters with two outright denials of the scream, attributing it successively to the Joven's imagination and to sensory deception, a phenomenon he proceeds to "prove" by scratching his ear and commenting in metaphorical terms on the sound produced by the scratching, which of course the Joven does not hear. The Ujier then deflects the Joven's final attempt to assert the reality of the scream by changing the topic of discussion to the Joven's choice of words. In this case the move from affirmation to the contradictory extreme of denial and finally to a meta-linguistic assertion that shifts the focus of attention away from the referent to language itself occurs within a single class of illocutionary acts, representatives.

A different type of contradictory illocutionary logic is illustrated by the Ujier's demand that the Joven open the door to his room from the inside when it is locked from the outside (25-26). This command violates the most important preparatory condition for directives, that is, that the hearer is able to do the act and that the speaker believes the hearer is able to do the act (Searle, *Speech Acts*, 66). The sincerity condition, that the speaker wants the hearer to do the act, seems to be violated here as well, but this is the case with most of the Funcionario's and the Ujier's illocutionary utterances in *Las paredes*. In any event, the Ujier's logic prevails by virtue of his superior position in the hierarchy of power:

JOVEN ... ¡Sabe usted bien que la puerta estaba cerrada por fuera!
UJIER (*secamente*) No, yo no sé nada. Usted sospecha que yo le gasté una broma, no adivino el fin, yo sospecho de usted: estamos a mano. ¡Y yo tengo razon! (26)

The Funcionario, whose elegant appearance and jovial manner contrast sharply with his role as an intimidating power figure, enters the Joven's room only occasionally. With an authority obviously superior to that of the Ujier, he dominates all speech exchanges and imposes his will categorically. In his first appearance, he talks incessantly, cutting off all attempts by the Joven to respond. In the midst of his chatter he abruptly turns to the Joven:

> FUNCIONARIO ¡Pero hable usted un poco! Parezco un charlatán. (con alarma) ¿Lo intimido, acaso? Míreme en los ojos. ¡Ay! Me sentiría muy herido (14).

The Funcionario performs, in rapid succession, a series of conflicting illocutionary acts: 1) an abrupt command that the Joven do what he has not been permitted to do, 2) an ironic act of self-representation, 3) a question expressing concern about his own intimidating manner, 4) a command that is obviously designed to intimidate, and 5) another ironic expression of his own sensitivity, presumably to accusations that he intimidates. The Funcionario's quick-fire alternation between the illocutionary categories of directives and representatives that slide toward expressives sends conflicting signals to the Joven: Don't talk / Talk; I don't wish to intimidate you / I attempt to intimidate you. The contradictory logic has a disorienting effect on the Joven, who responds with tentative, incomplete sentences.

The Funcionario uses a similar contradictory logic to thwart the Joven's attempt to counter the absurd accusation that he is Ruperto de Hentzau, an evil character from Anthony Hope's novel *The Prisoner of Zenda* (Cypess, "The Plays," 107, n. 9). The Funcionario intervenes as the Joven reaches for his billfold to produce indentification papers:

> FUNCIONARIO (lo detiene) ¡No necesito documentos! ¡Faltaría mas! Su palabra basta. (Suspira) (¡Qué alegría! Que por un azar del destino usted pudiera resultar Ruperto de Hentzau me quitaba el sueño. La averiguación demorará unos días (18).

The Funcionario's announcement of an investigation that will last several days contradicts his own assurances that the Joven's word is sufficient proof of his identity.

Such paradoxical logic violates the notion of illocutionary commitment investigated by Vanderveken, who notes that "The successful performance of an illocutionary act usually commits the speaker to other illocutionary acts. For example, a speaker who denies that it is raining is committed to asserting that it is not raining. A speaker who orders a hearer to stay and to do something is committed to granting him permission to stay" (249). The Funcionario's announcement of an investigation invalidates his expressed commitment to the truth value of the Joven's word. In setting contradictory conditions of success for his illocutionary acts, the Funcionario uses the logic of the "self-defeating illocutionary acts" described by Vanderveken, who adduces as examples such sentences as "I order and prohibit you from doing this," I promist [sic] not to keep this promise," and "I order you to disobey all orders" (249). The imposition of such logic by an authority figure on a subordinate places the latter in a double bind, or "a psychological dilemma in which a usually dependent person (as a child) receives conflicting interpersonal communication from a single source or faces disparagement no matter what his response to a situation" (*Webster's New Collegiate Dictionary*, 1979). Psychological studies cited by Norrick show that mild double-bind situations occurring in everyday conversation can cause a person to "become tongue-tied, stutter or blurt out something he immediately regrets," and that repeated imposition of double-bind situations on dependent persons can cause more serious psychological disorders (37).

Conflicting directives from the Funcionario and the Ujier are a frequent source of double-bind situations for the Joven. On one occasion, for example, the Funcionario steals the Joven's watch and brazenly displays it in his presence. Later, when the Ujier asks to borrow the watch "por algunos años," the Joven, afraid for obvious reasons to denounce the Funcionario, can only insist that he has lost it. The Ujier finds it absurd that the Joven could lose a watch in such a small room, and accuses him of lying. Here the Joven is faced with the dilemma of obeying either the implicit directive never to criticize the Funcionario, or the explicit contradictory directive to tell the truth about the watch. Although the Joven responds to this double-bind as logically as possible, disobeying the directive of the less powerful tormentor, the Ujier administers a beating (46-47). This is the only instance in the play in which physical punishment is actually inflicted on the Joven, although the threat of physical abuse is always in the background, reinforcing the obvious hierarchy of power.

The second category of manipulative tactics examined here is the Funcionario's and the Ujier's subversion of language's capacity to communicate. The tormentors use inappropriate vocabulary throughout the play to describe the Joven's situation. They refer to the prisoners as "nuestros huéspedes" (20), and to the Joven's confinement as "nuestro contrato social" (12). As in the first category, theatrical effects work in conjunction with dialogue to negate language's communicative value. The Funcionario and the Ujier frequently contradict and deny the reality of both audible and visual effects (the scream and the shrinking room, for example).

Often the Funcionario and the Ujier object to or comment on the Joven's use of language in order to change the subject of the dialogue from the referent to the medium of expression, as noted in the opening scene cited below. The Funcionario frequently uses foreign phrases, mainly French and Italian, when he wishes to make light of, or draw attention away from, a matter of concern to the Joven:

FUNCIONARIO ... Usted no está en situación de tentarse de risa.

JOVEN (lívido) ¿No estoy en situación?

FUNCIONARIO (sonríe instantáneamente) Porque su situación no es grave ni jocosa: "entièrement normal." ¿Qué tal mi francés, señor? Lo estudié con Madame Ninón de Lenclos. (Espía al joven que, obviamente, no conoce a Ninón de Lenclos) (38).

Here the Funcionario makes an ominous reference to the Joven's situation and uses the French as a pretext to interrupt his attempt to elicit clarification. At other times the Funcionario's foreign expressions are obviously designed to impede communication:

FUNCIONARIO ... ¿Quiere saber como marcha su asunto, "l'af-faire"?

JOVEN Sí, por favor.

FUNCIONARIO (alegre y ampuloso) "¡Laissez faire!"

JOVEN No... no entiendo.

FUNCIONARIO (ufano) ¿Por qué no estudia? El porvenir pertenece a los que estudian idiomas. Le hice una comunicación de interés, ¿y con qué resultado? ¡Ninguno! (50).

The communicative value of a foreign language that the hearer does not understand is equivalent to that of no language at all, as the Funcionario himself implies during his first visit to the Joven's room:

FUNCIONARIO ... Pero todo será para bien. "Tutto per bene," ¿no? Puede retirarse, ujier. Yo hablaré con el joven. La juventud habla mi idioma. (Divertido) ¡Yo no hablo ninguno! (13).

The Funcionario and the Ujier frequently subvert language's referential force by denying the distinction between dissimilar and sometimes antithetical terms. Thus, when the Joven states that he is twenty-two years old in response to the Funcionario's inquiry, the latter replies: "Lo advertí en seguida, le daba veinte o cuarenta, ni uno más" (37). The implied agreement of the first clause is immediately negated by the absurd doubling of years in the second. The effect is to deny the meaning of the Joven's words. In addition, the Funcionario's use of the idiomatic "le daba" suggests his own arbitrary powers to assign qualities. Later in the same conversation the following exchange takes place:

> JOVEN (*tímidamente*) Precisaba unas camisas, una muda de
> ropa. Claro que si mañana puedo salir en libertad...
> FUNCIONARIO (*risueño*) Puede salir, puede entrar, colita no vale...
> Puede quedarse con la ropa sucia hasta mañana,
> hasta pasado, hasta mil años (41).

Rather than denying outright the Joven's request for a change of
clothes, or refusing to respond to his tentative inquiry as to the status
of his detention, the Funcionario denies the elementary distinctions
(*salir, entrar; mañana, pasado, mil años*) on which the request and inquiry
are based.

An exchange between the Ujier and the Joven best illustrates the
denial of the distinction between dissimilar terms. The Ujier first
places the Joven in a typical double bind by telling him 1) his two-day
growth of beard is repugnant (the Ujier himself has an unkempt
beard of several days), 2) he cannot be released unless he is well-
groomed, 3) the detention center cannot provide shaving facilities,
and 4) the money the Joven has given him does not suffice to buy the
needed equipment. The following dialogue ensues:

> UJIER ... En la casa hemos tenido pocas oportunidades de
> servir a caballeros con ocurrencias tan peregrinas
> como las suyas.
> JOVEN ¿Como las mías? No entiendo.
> UJIER Sí, caballeros que pensaran en afeitarse antes de ...
> (*guarda un silencio significativo*)
> JOVEN (*palidece*) ¿Antes? Dijo "antes." ¿Antes de qué?
> UJIER (*con una sonrisa estúpida*) ¿Yo dije antes? ¡Qué extraño!
> Es una palabra que no uso nunca: le tengo tirria. Si
> preciso decir antes, digo después. Mis actos me
> siguen siempre a la zaga, retardados. Después de
> acostarme, digo, iré a dar una vuelta.
> JOVEN (*bajo*) Dijo antes.
> UJIER (*como si no entendiera*) No, no. Nunca voy antes. Me
> acuesto, duermo un rato y después paseo, lúcido,
> rozagante. Así concilio, con una fractura de tiempo,
> el lenguaje con mis actos (23).

The Joven apparently takes the incomplete sentence of the Ujier as an
ominous reference, perhaps to his death. When he tries to press the
point, however, the Ujier does several things: 1) he denies using the
word (*antes*) that the Joven demands he clarify, 2) he declares the
interchangeability of *antes* with *después*, or more precisely, the habitual
substitution of *después* for *antes* in his own speech, 3) he asserts a
disjuncture between his language and his acts, and 4) in performing
1), 2), and 3), he directs the topic of the discourse away from the

meaning of *antes* in this particular utterance to a generalization about his customary idiosyncratic use of the term. The Ujier's assertion of a time lapse between his speech and his acts that can only be reconciled by substituting one preposition or adverb for another that expresses an antithetical temporal relation, is particularly interesting from the perspective of speech-act theory, which is based on the premise that speaking and acting are simultaneous events. The Ujier's denial of this simultaneity can be seen as an attempt to undermine a fundamental human concept of the relationship between language and reality, the most radical instance of language subversion in *Las paredes*.

The negation of the referential value of words is paralleled in the denial of the truth value of representative statements. The Funcionario tells the Joven, for example, that the Ujier "estará a su entera disposición" and the Ujier later insists that this statement is a "figura literaria" (21). When the Joven turns pale and asks for clarification after the Ujier casually remarks that everyone at the detention center ends up in the boiler, the Ujier dismisses his phrase as "una forma de decir, bastante ordinaria, por cierto" (28).

The Funcionario and the Ujier also insist that the Joven modify his own statements to conform to their version of reality. The Ujier changes the Joven's statement "Me han traído" to "Usted se ha llegado hasta nosotros," and when the Joven insists "Me obligaron," the Ujier counters "Lo invitaron" (11). The Joven accepts these modifications and is careful to use the Ujier's suggested phraseology in subsequent references to his detainment.

The negation of the truth value of representative illocutionary acts is paralleled by the failure to fulfill the obligations assumed in the performance of commissive illocutionary acts. The Funcionario and the Ujier renege on promises they make throughout the play.[3] Often they are explicit in the disavowal of their commitments, as when the Ujier says of the Funcionario: "Le prometió venir mañana, le traerá buenas noticias. En caso contrario, desaparece. Promete venir y desaparece" (44).

---

[3] Although they are made in bad faith, they are still promises. As Austin notes, "In the particular case of promising, as with many other performatives, it is appropriate that the person uttering the promise should have a certain intention, viz. here to keep his word: and perhaps of all concomitants this looks the most suitable to be that which 'I promise' does describe or record. Do we not actually, when such intention is absent, speak of a 'false' promise? Yet so to speak is *not* to say that the utterance 'I promise that...' is false, in the sense that though he states that he does, he doesn't, or that though he describes he misdescribes—misreports. For he *does* promise: the promise here is not even *void*, though it is given *in bad faith*" (11). Similarly, Searle states that "insincere promises are promises nonetheless" ("What is a Speech Act?" 152).

The Joven is neither ingenuous nor an incompetent speaker or hearer. Though he attempts to clarify ambiguous statements, to make explicit the meaning of veiled threats, and to hold the Funcionario and Ujier responsible for the obligations they assume in their promises, he is consistently thwarted by diversionary tactics. As the play progresses, the Joven adopts the only counter-strategy available to him: he adapts to the rules of the game as he perceives them and begins to interpret promises as threats, threats as promises.[4] The Funcionario uses equivocal language during his final visit to the Joven's room, but his departing words are anything but subtle; "La vida es sueño. Y la muerte. No se asuste. Sólo le costará un poco soñarla... Hasta mañana, hijo, hasta mañana. Aunque mañana ya no nos veremos. ¡Quién sabe!" (51). The Joven interprets this as a promise that he will be released the following day. When the Ujier insinuates that such is not the case, the Joven's response is "¿Qué pasa? ¿Adelantaron la fecha? ¿Saldré hoy?" (54).

In the final scene the Ujier, after considerable prodding, cheerfully announces that the walls will collapse on the Joven at midnight. Although the Ujier repeats this bit of news several times, the Joven insists he is lying, and announces his plans to return to his job and to go on an excursion to the country the following Sunday. As the Ujier prepares to exit for the final time, the Joven detains him:

> JOVEN ¡Escúcheme! Me... me prometío comunicarme una noticia.
> UJIER (se detiene, con negligencia) ¡Le comuniqué tantas!
> JOVEN ¿Me ha mentido?
> UJIER ¡Sí, sí! "La verdad sospechosa." (Ríe)
> JOVEN (con obstinada decisión) El domingo iré al campo (60).

The allusion to Alarcón's famous comedia and to the refrán "En la boca mentirosa es la verdad sospechosa" is the Ujier's announcement of yet another change in the rules of the game. Whether one understands the Joven's impending death in the literal sense or figuratively, as the irreparable destruction of his identity and ability to act independently, it now appears that the Ujier is telling the truth. The Joven, however, has been deceived so often he can no longer distinguish between the truth and falsity of representative utterances, or the sincerity and insincerity of commissive utterances. In a final reversal, the Ujier assures the Joven that he will go to the country on Sunday and exits. Although he leaves the

---

[4] As Searle points out, promises and threats, though structurally very similar, differ in one crucial respect: "... a promise is a pledge to do something for you, not to you; but a threat is a pledge to do something to you, not for you" (Speech Acts, 58).

door to the room open, the Joven simply stares ahead and awaits his fate.

The Funcionario and the Ujier rely on the two classes of verbal tactics examined in this study, contradictory illocutionary logic and the subversion of language as a coherent system of communication, to achieve absolute control over the Joven's behavior. These categories, however, are not independent of one another. In an important sense, the first class subsumes the second. A basic category of illocutionary logic is Searle's principle of the "direction of illocutionary fit," according to which the point of representative utterances, on the one hand, is to get the speaker's words to match the world, and the point of commissive and directive utterances, on the other, is to get the world to match the speaker's words ("Classification," 3-4). The Funcionario and the Ujier consistently reverse the logic of this principle. In assigning antithetical meanings to words or reversing the truth value of representative utterances, they create their own versions of the world to fit their words. In their disavowal of the obligatory element of commissive utterances, they fail to make the world fit their words. This type of contradictory illocutionary logic, then, in large measure comprises the subversion of language in Las paredes.

The abuse of language, its use as a tool of coercion, deception, and behavioral manipulation in Las paredes, has important political implications. As in Orwell's 1984, subversion of the function of language is a primary means of exercising control over human behavior. The Joven's passive acceptance of his fate in the final scene is much the same as the "learned helplessness" of experimental subjects who are unable to take advantage of opportunities to flee after being subjected to inescapable forms of punishment (Dember, 700). In subverting the power of language, the Funcionario and the Ujier assert their own power to control, shape, and define reality according to their purposes or perhaps to a larger design of the State, implied in the totalitarian microcosm of Las paredes.

UNIVERSITY OF SCRANTON

Works Cited

Austin, J. L. How To Do Things With Words. 2nd ed. Cambridge, Mass.: Harvard University Press, 1962.

Carballido, Emilio. "Griselda Gambaro o modos de hacernos pensar en la manzana." Revista Iberoamericana 36 (1970): 629-34.

Cypess, Sandra Messinger. "Physical Imagery in the Works of Griselda Gambaro." Modern Drama 18 (1975): 357-64.

————. "The Plays of Griselda Gambaro." In *Dramatists in Revolt: The New Latin American Theater*. Ed. Leon F. Lyday and George W. Woodyard. Austin: University of Texas Press, 1976, 95-109.

Dauster, Frank. "Social Content and Revolutionary Form: Spanish American Drama Today." In *Ibero-American Letters in a Comparative Perspective*. Comparative Literature Symposium, Texas Tech University. Lubbock, TX: Texas Tech Press, 1978, pp. 49-63.

Dember, William N., et al. *General Psychology*. 2nd ed. Hillsdale, NJ: Lawrence Erlbaum Associates, 1984.

Elam, Keir. *The Semiotics of Theatre and Drama*. New York: Methuen & Co., 1980.

Foster, David William. "The Texture of Dramatic Action in the Plays of Griselda Gambaro." *Hispanic Journal* 1 (1980): 57-66.

Gambaro, Griselda. *Las paredes, El desatino, Los siameses*. Buenos Aires: Argonauta, 1979.

Gerdes, Dick. "Recent Argentine Vanguard Theatre: Gambaro's *Información para extranjeros*." *Latin American Theatre Review* 11 (1978): 11-16.

Hancher, Michael. "The Classification of Cooperative Illocutionary Acts." *Language in Society* 8 (1979): 1-14.

Holzapfel, Tamara. "Griselda Gambaro's Theatre of the Absurd." *Latin American Theatre Review* 4 (1970): 5-11.

Norrick, Neal R. "Nondirect Speech Acts and Double Binds." *Poetics* 10 (1980): 33-47.

Picón Garfield, Evelyn. "Una dulce bondad que atempera las crueldades: *El campo* de Gambaro." *Latin American Theatre Review* 13 (1980): 95-102.

Podol, Peter L. "Reality Perception and Stage Setting in Griselda Gambaro's *Las paredes* and Antonio Buero Vallejo's *La fundación*." *Modern Drama* 24 (1981): 44-53.

Postma, Rosalea. "Space and Spectator in the Theatre of Griselda Gambaro: *Información para extranjeros*." *Latin American Theatre Review* 14 (1980): 35-45.

Pratt, Mary Louise. "The Ideology of Speech-Act Theory." *Centrum* 1 (1981): 5-18.

Savona, Jeannette Laillou. "*Didascalies* as Speech Act." *Modern Drama* 25 (1982): 25-35.

Searle, John R. "A Classification of Illocutionary Acts." *Language in Society* 5 (1976): 1-23.

————. *Speech Acts: An Essay in the Philosophy of Language*. London: Cambridge University Press, 1969.

————. "What Is a Speech Act?" In *Language and Context*. Ed. Pier Paolo Giglioli. Baltimore: Penguin Books Inc., 1972, pp. 136-54.

Vanderveken, Daniel. "Illocutionary Logic and Self-Defeating Speech Acts." In *Speech Act Theory and Pragmatics*. Ed. John R. Searle, Ferenc Kiefer, and Manfred Bierwisch. Dordrecht, Holland: D. Reidel Publ. Co., 1980, pp. 247-272.

Speech Acts And Irony
In Two Plays Of Social Protest
By Sergio Vodanovic

PAUL CHRISTOPHER SMITH

I

 ERGIO VODANOVIC is a Chilean playwright born in 1926 who has enjoyed the popular success of several comedies, but his international reputation to date is based on his plays that attack social and political corruption. He became better known in the United States when the full-length *Deja que los perros ladren* (1959) and the one-act *El delantal blanco* (1974) were anthologized.[1] Both plays criticize hypocrisies that are only too common and well established in Latin America. Vodanovic insists that endeavors of Latin American theatre cannot be separated from the sociopolitical reality from which they emerge, and he has expressed dismay at U. S. drama critics who, in his view, fail to comprehend the complexities of Latin American societies. They mistakenly apply the criteria of Broadway and Paris for their own sense of universality ("Review Essay").[2] Vodanovic's observation, together with the political content of the two plays most widely read in the U. S., could lead one to

---

[1] In Castillo and Castillo, and Dauster and Lyday, respectively. All citations from *Deja* will be from the Castillo and Castillo edition. *Deja* is also available in Vodanovic, *Teatro*, which is reviewed by Agosin, ("Review"). Criticism on Vodanovic is limited. See Layera, "After," and Layera, "Contemporary"; also Vidal for an historical-economical reading of *Deja*.

[2] Vodanovic reiterated this opinion in a recent interview, asserting that he has not even been interested in how his plays are interpreted abroad. He declares that what does matter to him is communicating with an audience that he knows and a society he knows (Agosin, "Entrevista" 69).

suspect Vodanovic of being a rigid leftist that will not tolerate a concept of literature or theatre that does not promote social change. Such is not the case however, for while Vodanovic declares the playwright's community to be the fundamental criterion with which to begin judgment of a Latin American play, his own plays show that corruption as a theme is more central to his work than any particular political persuasion. His plays foreground various human characteristics that reveal corruption to be the genuinely complex phenomenon that it is; they do not oversimplify complicated social problems as codified good and evil systems with clearly delineated villains and victims.

Igual que antes, written in 1972-73, is a Vodanovic play in which corruption is thematic as well,[3] but here it comes from a community living in supposedly successful socialism achieved by open elections. (The overthrow and death of Allende was in September, 1973.) The protagonist of this play and that of *Deja que los perros ladren* are at opposite extremes from each other personally, professionally and politically, yet both become overwhelmed by corruption in very different ways. One fights it and the other promotes it; one finally recognizes its effects and reacts, while the other is oblivious until it is too late. What they do have in common is the importance of their families. Vodanovic makes these plays with obvious sociopolitical content more complete by intergrating the importance and nature of the politics into the makeup of the families. It is by the protagonists' own words—declarations about themselves, about their families, and about their particular sociopolitical situations—that the individual as individual, the individual as part of a family unit, and the individual as part of a society are all intertwined in a cohesive dramatic unit. Furthermore, the main characters' words provide a play-long network of self-descriptive and self-defining observations that lead to the ironic states of reversal and belated awareness.

Peter Dunn has recently demonstrated how irony is inseparable from whatever other features amount to a play's structure, and how "local" ironies become a part of the deep structure of a play. The conflicts of irony lead us toward peripeteia, but, if it surprises us, as Dunn says, "the turn of events is always expected—with hindsight." "The *peripeteia* is not *part* of the play on the same level on which a speech or an event is part of a play; rather it *is* the play experienced as movement, and in it all the local ironies are incorporated" ("Irony" 321). (The emphases are Dunn's.) The speeches of an ironic play, then, are parts that contribute to the local ironies and the deeper

---

³ This play is not published, but it has been performed in Chile and adapted for television by Vodanovic. It has been translated and published in English by Ramón Layera (Same). I am indebted to Professor Layera for a copy of the Spanish manuscript, from which all citations will be taken.

structure, and the task of the playwright is to weave them all together in a fashion that allows for the play to be experienced as movement which is both cohesive and dramatic. It is, I propose, precisely this relationship among speech, local irony, and the entire structure of a play that can be elucidated by applying recent speech-act theory. The theory is a promising tool for the analysis of dramatic discourse to show, for example, how the local ironies are incorporated by means of the sentences that bear them, how and why certain utterances are more significant than others, and how characters by means of these utterances shape events, other characters, and even themselves. These kinds of speech acts occur frequently in *Deja que los perros ladren* and *Igual que antes*. If further justification should be needed for the application of speech-act theory to theatre, we need only ask ourselves what we mean when we speak of the action of a play. Traditionally we think of events both on and off stage, acts we see, characters' movements, and so on. However, in both classical and contemporary theatre, slaps, blows, swoons, falls, fights, and deaths, are, after all, rare indeed when seen against their linguistic backdrop of dialogic exchange. The essential "action" in most plays is in the speech acts: arguments, promises, threats, declarations, assertions, lies, deceptions.

Speech-act theory has its origins in philosopher John Austin's observations on certain types of utterances he called performatives in which "the doing is in the saying." (Baptizing, for example, or a judge declaring the "Court is now in session.") John Searle and others have refined Austin's ideas, and there are now several efforts to apply this theory of language as action to literary discourse.[4] A concise yet thorough introduction to speech-act theory and its potential for the analysis of dramatic texts is found in Keir Elam, *The Semiotics of Theatre and Drama*. Searle has identified the following types of speech acts:

the utterance act is the uttering of morphemes and sentences; the propositional act refers and predicates; the illocutionary act is the act performed in saying something (asserting, questioning, ordering); and the perlocutionary act, which is the act performed by means of saying something (persuading, inspiring, convincing or angering). (Elam, 158)

This last act depends on the effect of the utterance; if the interlocutor is persuaded or angered, that is the perlocutionary effect. The

---

4 See Austin's seminal *How*, and Searle. Pratt ("Ideology") is important for her attempt to apply speech-act theory broadly to literary discourse (see also Traugott and Pratt, *Linguistics*), and Fish is equally important for his caution against trying to stretch the theory beyond what he sees as its limitations.

illocutionary force of a speech act and its possible perlocutionary effect are certainly central to what we see and hear on stage.

Three felicity conditions have been established which govern the performance of illocutionary acts and determine whether they are successful or defective:

> to fulfill the preparatory condition, the speaker must have the authority to perform the act;
> to fulfill the sincerity condition, he must believe what he says to be true, he must want what he requests;
> to fulfill the essential condition the utterance must count as some type of commitment or endeavor. (Elam, *Semiotics* 162-63)

(A judge has the authority to open a court session—a defendant does not; both a judge and a defendant can sincerely express desires for rehabilitation; a judge is committed by his words when he sentences or grants parole, and a defendant may oblige himself by promising behavior appropriate to being released on bond or granted parole.) In addition to the infelicitous possibilities that may make a speech act defective, the illocutionary force of a speech act may fall on figurative deaf ears. Without the "securing of uptake," in Austin's words, the intended illocutionary act is unlikely to succeed. This is frequent in comedy, of course, when dialogic exchange occurs at different levels and we then see ludicrous consequences. There can also be a breakdown between what the sentence means and what the utterer means, and this applies not only to the character on stage that hears the sentence, but to the readers of dramatic texts and viewers of plays as well. The function of a sentence may be strikingly different from its form. When Don Juan says "I promise to marry you," the form is understood by his listener and he secures uptake, but the audience is fully aware that the function of the language is deception. He fulfills neither the sincerity nor the essential condition. (In simpler daily language, "Is the radio too loud?" may be a simple question, but it could also be an assertion or even a threat, and a response of "Yes" might be problematical.)

II

Let us now turn to the two Vodanovic plays and examine the role of speech acts in the shaping of characters and irony. In *Deja que los perros ladren* Esteban is a naïve middle-level functionary who believes in—and acts and speaks according to—the bureaucratic system that has conditioned him. He is a good model for one of Searle's early points of departure: "To perform illocutionary acts is to engage in a rule-governed form of behavior" (in Giglioli, *Language* 137). The essence of the play is Esteban's resistance to corruption, his succumbing to it and thus seeing his son corrupted as well, and the final rebellion and return to his earlier honesty but without the earlier naïveté. The opening scene has one confirmation after another of a belief in order, regulations, and family unity. Esteban's son, Octavio, has no doubts about his future: "Seguiré la tradición familiar y seré un abogodo como mi padre y como mi abuelo, saliendo bien en todos los exámenes." Rules for propriety and orderliness seem to govern Esteban, both professionally and personally. When his wife, Carmen, chides him for wearing a tie on a trip to the beach, he responds with a strange self-descriptive or self-defining illocutionary act:[5] "Es que yo no soy yo sin corbata." The self-image is so strong that he fails to understand at first the implication behind Carmen's "Todo lo contrario. Cuando estás sin corbata es cuando más me gustas." That is, he is slow on the uptake of this statement's illocutionary force.

The ethical issue that Esteban must face is presented in the first scene also. What the Ministro suggests is antithetical to Esteban's view of himself and the world. The Ministro first attempts to persuade Esteban to get a loan for a new house, but Esteban points out that he does not meet the requirements. The Ministro didn't even know there were certain requirements and he offers to circumvent them. Esteban's "Pero el reglamento..." is met with "Siempre eres el mismo. ¡Lo único que te importa son los reglamentos!" Esteban says he doesn't want to do anything wrong, but the Ministro poses a rhetorical question which later governs much of the behavior of both Esteban and Octavio: "¿Es incorrecto hacer lo que todos hacen?" The Ministro then gets to the real purpose of his visit which is to convince Esteban to close down a sensationalist newspaper (supposedly because of bad sanitary conditions) that is critical of the government. When Esteban protests, "Me estás pidiendo que abuse de mis funciones," the Ministro flippantly responds with a cliché, "El jefe que no abusa, pierde su autoridad." The Ministro returns to the topic of the family, but now as a point of leverage, indicating to Esteban that if he should lose his job, it would hurt his wife and son. The scene ends with

---

[5] Searle's taxonomy of illocutionary acts, with examples by Elam, can be found in Elam (166-67):

1. *Representatives*, committing the speaker to the truth of the proposition asserted.
2. *Directives*, attempts to get the listener to do something, whether it be to perform a deed, to give the speaker something, or simply to provide information...
3. *Commissives*, committing the speaker to a future course of action...
4. *Expressives*, conventional acts such as thanking, greeting, congratulating, whose sincerity conditions include a particular psychological state...
5. *Declarations*, those acts which, if performed "happily," actually bring about the state of affairs proposed...

another manifestation of order for both family and society. Octavio downplays the importance of class in theory of law and Esteban reacts for two reasons: he wants his son to believe in the importance of law, and he has just been asked by a superior to commit an unethical act. For Esteban the law "Es el único medio para evitar el abuso, el abuso del físicamente más poderoso, del económicamente más poderoso..." The law provides order for himself and for his world, and both have been threatened by the Ministro. Reciting the words of the law seems to strengthen his shaken convictions. In speech-act terminology, his recitation—similar to the recitation of a sacred text—is an attempt to make "the world fit the words," even though he is already preoccupied with the truth or status of the words (the far more common use of words is a representative manner in which words are made to fit, or represent, the world).

The more pivotal developments of the first act continue to be Esteban's speech acts which name deeds or people, or which assert his own identity or images:

No sé mentir.

... la ley me protege. Nada me puede suceder si obro de acuerdo con la ley.

... tengo la impresión de ser tan poca cosa... Le parezco ingenuo. La familia que yo he hecho a mi imagen y semejanza.

Siempre me he vangloriado de respetar la ley. Creía que ahí estaba mi fortaleza, pero ésa es mi debilidad.

These self-defining speech acts show the progression of his succumbing to the Ministro's threats and bribes. He decides to join the corrupt power system and lay aside his former beliefs and identity.

The second act reveals a wealthy Esteban, now so concerned with money-making schemes that he virtually has lost sight of his son who has become an assistant to the Ministro. Octavio has quit school and is dedicated to the quick, easy life with no scruples whatsoever, even to the point of teasing his father about a call from a woman. Whereas Esteban had rationalized the compromising of his earlier convictions as action on behalf of his son and wife, he now realizes that Octavio is totally corrupted and that he was the model for him. Esteban's language is again that of image-making, and now self-blame: "¿Qué he hecho de ti? ¿Éste es el hombre que yo he formado?" The ultimate irony and proof of his son's moral demise is when Octavio calls Esteban "ingenuo" as his friends did formerly, but now he hears this name because Octavio is completely cynical and can't imagine Esteban's return to honesty. With his new-found commitment and self-awareness, and without his former naïveté, he has decided to expose the Ministro's (and his own) illegal activities even though it may ruin his career. His effort is crushed, however, by the smear campaign that the power structure uses against him. Speaking later with the idealistic—but now also ruined—publisher of the newspaper in question earlier, all appears to be lost. The publisher spoke earlier of there being nothing for young people to believe in, yet Octavio is convinced belatedly, and volunteers to obtain concrete evidence against the Ministro which can be printed and used in court. We assume that the united and redefined father-son team will succeed.

The later *Igual que antes* is a much more theatrical work divided into eight scenes. The first reveals the rather hopeless state of Víctor's family. He, his wife Ana, and daughter Silvia are presented in a forced, awkward afternoon of pretending all is well. The photograph for which they pose with fake smiles is projected as the backdrop for the next seven scenes, which comprise an extended flashback showing how the family deteriorated and how out of touch Víctor is—out of touch with his wife, daughter, the employees of his factory, his accountant friend, and most significantly, himself. He declares himself to be the "new man," the model socialist, the perfect family man, and the irresistable lover. He abuses, however, the other party in each of these relationships. His initial declarative speech act, "Yo soy socialista," (later repetitions would be representatives) does meet the preparatory and indeed the sincerity conditions. He genuinely considers himself to be a socialist and to comply with all the other roles, and therefore his complete self-deception is gradually shown as the audience realizes he does not fulfill the essential condition. Whereas Esteban's ultimate "I am honest" fulfills all three felicity conditions after his floundering and rationalization, his earlier self-defining assertions do indicate that he knew he was "doing what everyone else does" while embezzling government funds. Víctor's irony is formed with self-defining speech acts also, but he is caught totally unaware when his imagined world, that is constructed of his words, only turns out to be the radically different world of the words of those around him. In this case he does make the world fit the words—but only for himself, and only for a limited time. It is only a matter of time until Víctor's behavior shows little or no similarity to what would be overt, public criteria for a socialist's behavior. The play consists of stripping away one self-deluded layer at a time.

The daughter, Silvia, and her boyfriend, Martín, also deceive themselves, again within the framework of a new, progressive society. They claim to be the promise of the future and criticize parents with typical generation-gap complaints. In the second scene they show how immature they really are; they are ignorant of certain basic biological matters concerning sex while they boast of their liberation and adulthood. Furthermore, they tease each other in a way that belies their observations. Their naïve and hypocritical proclamations set the tone for Víctor's in the next scene. He boasts, "¡Yo ya soy el hombre nuevo!" and sings student socialist songs, reminisces about university activism, and then, after his accountant informs him that his workers have denounced him, he makes the following remarks about them:

> Pero si son mis amigos... saben que soy de izquierda igual que ellos.
> ¡Hijos de perras!
> Eso lo arreglo de una patada. Les tiro unos pesos más y queda todo solucionado.
> Mis obreros son como hijos míos.

The same conversation later turns to family affairs, and when asked about Silvia, he declares, "Yo no tengo problemas," and adds that his daughter is the only thing of real importance to him. The accountant is less than convinced, but Víctor appears to have kept his world and image intact for the moment.

After a scene of excellent, hilarious parody by the young people mocking traditional but narrow-minded mores, Víctor is seen on a hunting trip with the accountant. His sexist declarations reveal attitudes that, in general, are inconsistent with socialist behavior but which do support his machista self-image. He has to force the door of a cabin, and, overgeneralizing about gender and the use of force, he reminds his friend that "el sustantivo *puerta* es feminino." Regarding women, he is convinced that, "Lo bueno es que yo les gusto a ellas." Further support for Víctor's image is his purported success with women, and as long as he succeeds with women he is confident: "... el día que falle con las mujeres, sabré que me llegó la hora." When two young women who were swimming nearby run to the cabin because of a storm, the men think of them as an opportunity to "make the world fit their previous, boasting words." The women, however, are able to make complete fools of them, and they flee, calling them "viejos impotentes." Víctor's friend accepts that as true, but Víctor insists "No oí nada," and prepares to use some women's clothing that was drying as proof of a conquest to other hunters.

The next two scenes are between Víctor and his daughter, and Víctor and his wife, during which his self-images of father and husband are destroyed. He doesn't want to accept Silvia's accusations of hypocrisy when he complains of her life-style. He finally, and limply, uses the same language that Silvia's immature boyfriend did earlier ("Al fin de cuentas soy un hombre...") when she reveals that she as well as her mother have known of his mistress for years. Any possible credence given to his observations like "Yo sé de estas cosas" (in reference to Silvia's relationship), and "Soy razonable" is steadily eroded, first by his own actions, and then by what others say about his public behavior. The words of others continue to break through his once invincible self-image by forcing him to recognize that he does not fulfill the essential condition of his many "I am..." declarations.

The scene with Ana opens with Víctor tearing up photographs. He is able to grasp, finally, that photographs can be false images: "... esas imágenes que por haberlas fotografiado creía que eran verdaderas y son tan sólo papel." But photographs are seen only occasionally while speech acts are articulated and heard continually. He seems unaware still that it was his various self-images plus their constant reinforcement by his own words that led to his self-deception and downfall. He is not the victim of others' plotting, (as he thinks at first), but of himself. Víctor is dumbfounded that Ana could have both known about his mistress and remained calm. Her resolve to maintain appearances and her well-being is again related to the power of words: "Nunca lo mencionamos, luego no existió. Si ahora lo nombramos es porque ya no existe."

What these words *do* cannot be placed in speech-act theory per se, but their function can be interpreted with the help of the theory when seen in a curious reverse manner. Ana insists on her ability to ignore, to *assert away* a particular piece of the world by not recognizing it with words, which in effect, is a "reverse declarative."[6] Giving adultery a name would cause it to exist in her world, so she chooses not to name it, thus keeping it from existing—for her. Now that she learns adultery no longer exists in Víctor's world, it can safely be mentioned since it therefore will not exist in hers either. This we call, of course, head-in-the-sand behavior, but her strength for this posturing is derived from her words (or the absence of them).

She sees the return of some previous happy state, "Y nada habrá cambiado." The play ends with a return to the opening pose for the photograph—the scene that has been projected during the other scenes. Ana's "Somos una familia feliz" functions the same as "Say cheese" does for purposes of photography, but it is also the last ironic, defective speech act of a play whose interest and unity are due, in

---

[6] Another interesting case of an "ambiguous declarative" that seems to slip between the cracks of the theory is when a parent "disowns" a child. "I disown you" or "I have no son" can indeed bring about a new world in which there is no functional relationship whatsoever between two people. A biological relationship necessarily continues, however. It would appear the "most difficult" essential felicity condition is fulfilled, as well as the sincerity condition. But is the preparatory? The point here is not to question the validity of speech-act theory, but rather to show how the theory can provide a heightened awareness of the subtleties of human interaction, which in turn is useful for literary analysis.

large part, to defective speech acts, acts of self-deception that foreshadow irony. They are not, however, defective dramatically—they supply the necessary preliminaries for Peter Dunn's "turn of events which is expected with hindsight."

The events turn with the speech acts because speech acts reflect the conventional behavior of societies, families, and individuals. In *Deja que los perros ladren* we have language that is a result of particular family and legal conventions which become undermined by illegal actions, or the "conventions" of corrupt politicians. The verbal declarations in *Igual que antes* also reflect familial and societal conventions. Both Esteban and Víctor "suffer" from self-image governed thought that leads to self-image promoting speech acts. Their words establish and maintain their identities as well as provide for a defense and preservation of the self, but they sometimes communicate only with themselves. As Stanley Fish has very perceptively summarized, "Speech-act theory is an account of the conditions of intelligibility, of what it means to mean in a community, of the procedures which must be instituted before one can even be said to be understood" ("How to" 1024). At the beginning of both plays, the characters appear to function successfully in family communties, and to one extent or another, Esteban succeeds in a community of laws and order, while Víctor succeeds in a community of socialism. The interesting theatre occurs with the ironic reversal of their circumstances brought about by their self-deception and their own words. Their respective ends are different, and while what the plays "say" is quite clear, the conclusions as well as the local ironies are elucidated by a speech-act interpretation. Esteban enjoys a classic victory in defeat, for there is uptake to his ultimate "I am an honest man." He acquires a higher level of intelligibility for himself and for his family, and he has new knowledge of what it means to mean in a society of law even though it is a society pressured by politicians' corruption. His most significant uptake is Octavio's return to honesty, the final perlocutionary effect. Víctor receives no final uptake to his "I am a socialist." He failed to be intelligible for his family, and he failed to comprehend what it means to mean in a socialist society. The irony of both protagonists develops from that part of their speech acts which is infelicitous. The defective, self-defining speech act leads to defective familial and societal relations, which lead in turn to dramatic reversal.

SOUTHERN ARKANSAS UNIVERSITY

Works Cited

Agosin, Marjorie. "Entrevista con Sergio Vodanovic." *Latin American Theatre Review* 17.2 (1984): 65-71.

————. Review of *Teatro*, by Sergio Vodanovic. *Latin American Theatre Review* 13.2 (1980): 99-101.

Austin, J. L. *How to Do Things with Words*. Ed. J. O. Urmson and Marina Sbisà. 2nd edition. Cambridge: Harvard University Press, 1975.

Dauster, Frank, and Leon F. Lyday. *En un acto. Nueve piezas hispanoamericanos*. New York: D. Van Nostrand, 1974.

Dunn, Peter N. "Irony as Structure in the Drama." *Bulletin of Hispanic Studies* 61.3 (1984): 317-25.

Elam, Keir. *The Semiotics of Theatre and Drama*. London: Methuen, 1980.

Fish, Stanley. "How to Do Things with Austin and Searle: Speech-Act Theory and Literary Criticism." *MLN* 91 (1976): 983-1025.

Layera, Ramón. "After the Coup: Four Dramatic Versions of Allende's Chile." *Latin American Theatre Review* 12.1 (1978): 39-42.

————. "Contemporary Spanish American Drama of Denunciation and Social Protest: The Case of Argentina and Chile." *DAI*, 38 (1977), 2102-A (SUNY at Binghamton).

Pratt, Mary Louise. "The Ideology of Speech-Act Theory," *Centrum New Series* 1.1 (1981): 5-18.

Searle, John. "What is a Speech Act?" In *Language and Social Context*. Ed. Pier Paolo Giglioli. London: Penguin Education, 1972, 136-54.

Traugott, Elizabeth Closs, and Mary Louise Pratt. *Linguistics for Students of Literature*. New York: Harcourt, Brace, Jovanovich, 1980.

Vidal, Hernán. "*Deja que los perros ladren* de Sergio Vodanovic: Desarrollismo, Democracia Cristiana, Dictadura." *Revista iberoamericana* 47 (1981): 313-35.

Vodanovic, Sergio. *Deja que los perros ladren*. In *Tres novelas cortas. Tres piezas teatrales*. Ed. Homero Castillo and Audrey G. Castillo. New York: Holt Rinehart and Winston, 1970.

————. *Igual que antes*. Unpublished manuscript, 1972-73.

————. *Same as Ever*. Trans. Ramón Layera. In *Modern International Drama* 12.1 (1978): 7-50.

————. *Teatro*. Santiago de Chile: Editorial Nascimiento, 1978.

————. "Theater in Society in Latin America." Trans. by Scott Lubeck. *Journal of Interamerican Studies and World Affairs* 18.4 (1976): 495-504.

On The Margins Of
Self-Conscious Discourse:
Reading and Writing As Conversation
In Mario Vargas Llosa's
La señorita de Tacna

SANDRA M. BOSCHETTO

HE PUBLICATION OF *La señorita de Tacna* in 1981 marks a change in the artistic trajectory of Mario Vargas Llosa. Whereas the previous works are novels of increasing structural complexity, this more recent accomplishment is the author's first published play.[1] Not unlike his previous narrative achievements, however, this playfully dialogic effort represents a continuation of the movement toward traditional storytelling with organizing principles that point to specific humorous and critical effects.

The publication and staging of *La señorita de Tacna*[2] should in no way be viewed as a mere marginal incursion into theatrical territory, but rather as a work in perfect harmony with the author's total artistic development. Indeed, the dramatist who first wrote and staged *La huida del inca* in 1952 at the age of 15 was never completely effaced. Although better known to his readers as a novelist and storyteller, Vargas Llosa has been characterized as a writer of dialogical narrations, narrative spirals in dialogue form, and pluridimensional

---

[1] Mario Vargas Llosa, *La señorita de Tacna* (Barcelona: Editorial Seix Barral, S. A., 1981). Subsequent quotes are from this edition.

[2] The play was first staged in Buenos Aires on April 27, 1981 at the Teatro Blanca Podestá. It has subsequently been staged in Mexico City and more recently in New York under the stage direction of Enrique Giordano.

narrations.[3] As one critic notes, "... este novelista ha logrado cristalizar una prosa que no es diálogo ni narración (ni descripción ni meditación) propiamente, sino una aleación, una fusión vitalizadora en que se narra dialogando, sin hablar, y se dialoga narrando, sin narrar."[4] The self-reflexive nature of Vargas Llosa's narrative is rendered through dialogical sequences and narrative configurations which dramatically draw the reader into the process of narration. The impression conveyed by Vargas Llosa's prose is that of narration "cimentada sobre una conversación."[5]

Although C. Lucía Garavito's article—the only published analysis of *La señorita de Tacna* thus far—is an enlightening contribution to criticism,[6] her study fails to earmark the play's theatrical conventions for special consideration. The present study, therefore, attempts to fill some of the gaps left by her investigation.

While certain structural constants of Vargas Llosa's prose are recognizable in the play,[7] the reader must not forget that major conventions which do belong to drama do not belong to narrative. Drama is designed for theatrical presentation; that is, although we speak of a drama as a literary work or a composition, drama is designed to be acted on the stage, is written to be spoken. This aspect of dramatic form is significant precisely because it serves to illustrate Vargas Llosa's conception of how discourse should work in the novel. In drama, we know nothing about the characters except what they tell us. That is, there is normally little or no narration or description in drama. Because this is so, the playwright must present his characters almost entirely through dialogue and action. Whereas in a novel the author can describe fully in an objective way, the only description of a character in a play are those made by other characters—and those descriptions usually tell us as much about the speaker as about the person to whom that speaker is referring. The narration in drama is hidden in the sense that it is not the "author's" direct comment. As Keir Elam explains: "The dialogue in drama is

---

[3] J. M. Oviedo, *Mario Vargas Llosa: la invención de una realidad* (Barcelona: Barral Editores, 1970), p. 231.

[4] José Luis Martín, *La narrativa de Vargas Llosa* (Madrid: Editorial Gredos, 1974), p. 209.

[5] *La narrativa de Vargas Llosa*, p. 209.

[6] C. Lucía Garavito, "*La señorita de Tacna* o la escritura de una lectura," *Latin American Theatre Review*, 16 (no. 1, Fall 1982), 3-14.

[7] These constants include the interior duplication scheme, or "cajas chinas"; narratives that intertwine two dialogues—one present, the other evoked and made present by the first—happening in two different moments of time and space, or "telescopic procedure"; and finally, the conjoining of fiction and verisimilitude, or what Vargas Llosa terms "salto cualitativo." See M. Vargas Llosa, *La novela* (Montevideo: Fundación de Cultura Universitaria, 1969), pp. 24-25, 26, 28.

immediate 'spoken action' rather than reference to, or representation of, action, so that the central personal, political, and moral oppositions which structure the drama are seen and heard to be acted out in the communicational exchange, and not described at a narrative remove... Illocutionary acts move the play along."[8]

La señorita de Tacna is original as a work of literature not only becuase it posits the convergence of drama and narrative, but more precisely because in the work narrative is viewed as drama. Just as the novels of Vargas Llosa create the impression of narrative founded upon conversation, so now La señorita de Tacna is inversely a verbal event, a conversation founded upon simultaneous acts of narration, "real," imagined, and imitated. If drama is a performance, then the play harbors another theme, that of reading and writing as performance, reading and writing as speaking. Finally, the work in both form and content posits a tension between spoken and written acts of narration.

The principal characters within the play, Belisario and Mamaé— who may be viewed as one collective character—are both fabulators in the process of fabulating,[9] one by means of the written word (Belisario as scribe), and the other through oral narration (Mamaé as storyteller, whose act of narration implies pure orality). Because of the ever-present focus on story, and more precisely on the act of narration, both oral and written, it is inaccurate to label the play as metatheatrical. The play, in fact, partakes of both genres, drama and narrative, and is hence more accurately labeled as metaliterature or metafiction. La señorita de Tacna is a play (emphasis on oral dialogue and theatrical communication) about a character-scribe who is in the process of attempting to compose a story about another story: the story of a storyteller (a product of the character-scribe's imaginative recollection) who is in the process of telling other stories. The play of imaginary voices in dialogue is, then, a central device for generating the text. This self-reflexive construction displays three organizing principles: 1) fiction as process not form, as communicative act not object; 2) reading and writing as speaking; and 3) the relationship between oral and written, nonliterary and literary narration.

---

[8] Keir Elam, The Semiotics of Theatre and Drama (Methven: London and New York, 1980), p. 162).

[9] A definition of fabulation is provided by Robert Scholes in Fabulation and Metafiction (Chicago: University of Illinois Press, 1980): "Fabulation... means not a turning away from reality, but an attempt to find more subtle correspondences between the reality which is fiction and the fiction which is reality. Modern fabulation accepts, even emphasizes, its 'fallibilism,' its inability to reach all the way to the real, but it continues to look toward reality" (p. 8).

ORAL NARRATIVE AND THE STORYTELLER

In La señorita de Tacna the imagined oral discourse of fictitious characters is used to replace the formal written discourse of an author's persona. The oral narrative structure and dramatic dialogue frame of the play highlight the preeminence of oral literature and performative orality (speakers and listeners engaged in communicative acts). As the play narrates the various steps in the construction of a story, so too, in metatheatrical fashion, it speaks ambiguously and with tongue in cheek of its own ambiguity and of its own derisory nature. La señorita de Tacna is a web of dialogized narratives framed by dramatic dialogue. The presentation of literature or poetic discourse as an oral art and as an oral act reduces distance and "defictionalizes" the speech situation. This manner of presenting literature also contributes to the blurring of distinctions between nonfiction and fiction, natural and so-called "poetic" narrative.

Vargas Llosa appears to acknowledge that literature was in the first place created by one person speaking to others and that this primal situation of oral performance is still being recreated or imitated by most literary works. The view of literature as performance, as communicative act, is central to Vargas Llosa's theory of literature. According to the author's philosophy of artistic creation, the "invisible storyteller," as he terms this speaking voice, creates a particular impression upon the reader, allowing him or her to experience "una intimidad, de estar escuchando, viendo, una conciencia en movimiento antes o sin necesidad de que se convierta en expresión oral, es decir, siente que comparte una subjetividad."[10] This conception of narrative is opposed to the theory which tends to view literary works as fixed objects.

One of the reasons critics have often tended to view literary works as objects rather than as communicative acts is that most literary works have the form of written texts. In this sense, they are objects in a way spoken discourses are not. In usual written discourse, "we have the curious situation that the speaker is unknown or known only by name to hearers, and the hearers are unknown to the speaker. The speaker/hearer relations are, thus, extremely depersonalized and abstract in comparison with face-to-face spoken discourse."[11] Taking discourse in life as a model for discourse in art, Vargas Llosa playfully undermines the status of literary works as artifacts. In La señorita de Tacna he posits an imaginary situation—a metatheatrical and metafictional performance—wherein speaker/hearer, writer/reader relationships are directly displayed. Such an

---

[10] Cited in "Vargas Llosa: Teoría y Praxis," Grial, 51 (1976), 27.
[11] Elizabeth Closs Traugott and Mary Louise Pratt, Linguistics for Students of Literature (New York: Harcourt Brace Jovanovich, Inc., 1980), p. 261.

attitude "dematerializes" literature, strives to reduce its material density *as* language, and connects it to the intimate spiritual encounter of living "persons."

La señorita de Tacna begins with an invitation, or more appropriately an exhortation, to witness the power of the spoken word. Mamaé, the centenarian storyteller, is about to verbalize the act of creation:

> MAMAÉ   Los ríos, se salen los ríos... El agua, la espuma, los globitos, la lluvia lo está empapando todo, se vienen las olas, se está chorreando el mundo, la inundación, se pasa el agua, se sale, se escapa. Las cataratas, las burbujas, el diluvio, los globitos, el río... ¡Ayyy! (21).

The Biblical references to the Flood point more essentially to the generative power of the spoken word, to a kind of myth of literary autogenesis in which oral narrative takes on the fluid, spontaneous sprawling consistency of life itself. "La palabra viva," as one critic says, "la palabra preñada de suspenso, de magnética sugestión, la palabra cósmica de la creación original—'en el principio fue el Verbo'—la palabra como alfa y omega de la obra literaria."[12] The listener/reader is caught up in the storyteller's act of attention, which arouses expectations of tale-telling. This very first manifestation of language as simultaneous act of narration and creation posits the idealization of reality, the actualization of possible worlds or possible states of affairs through the imagination. The recreative power of the storyteller's language will transform Mamaé's "charco de pis" into "Diluvio."

The first level of fictionalization in *La señorita de Tacna* corresponds to the invention of Mamaé's own history—that of a young girl in love with a handsome Chilean officer. On her wedding day she learns that her husband-to-be has been seeing another woman, "Señora Carlota," with whom he is passionately in love. After suffering the typical "desengaño," Elvira decides to forego marriage and is invited to share family life with her cousin, her cousin's husband and their children. Mamaé devoted herself to telling stories to her nieces and nephews. As Belisario will do later, she modifies certain autobiographical details with the aid of imagination and by force of appropriate social and literary conventions. The listener/reader, therefore, is unable to distinguish the factual from the recreated or purely invented.

Mamaé engages in conversation with several characters in the play. Although narratives and stories are usually thought of as one and the same, that is, as functioning within the realm of strict "poetic discourse," not all narrative utterances are stories in this strict sense.

---

[12] *La narrativa de Vargas Llosa*, p. 245.

Stories are usually distinguished by the fact that they are an utterance type used when one is "recapitulating experience for display purposes, rather than for simple information-giving purposes or for some other purpose."[13] Stories, therefore, may also be detected in ordinary conversations. As one critic explains: "conversation is typically thought of in nonliterary terms. However, it plays an important role in literature, especially prose fiction and drama, where it is usually termed dialogue... Students of literature tend to think of narrative as a literary genre typical of prose fiction or epic poetry. Narrative is found in a wide number of contexts, including conversation."[14] As the characters in *La señorita de Tacna* converse about their ordinary, everyday happenings, their discourse becomes contaminated with poetic markings: these characters are not speaking so much to inform as to display. An example is the conversation between Elvira-Mamaé and the Abuela which takes place following the former's decision not to marry Joaquín:

> ABUELA (Entrando) ¡Elvira! ¡Elvira! ¡Pero qué has hecho! ¿Te has vuelto loca? ¡Pero cómo es posible! ¡Tu vestido de novia! ¡Tan lindo, todo bordado de encaje, con su velo que parecía espuma!
>
> MAMAÉ Me costó media caja de fósforos y quemarme las yemas de los dedos. Por fin se me occurió echarle un poco de parafina. Así ardió.
>
> ABUELA Pero si la boda es mañana. Si la gente está viniendo para el matrimonio desde Moquegua, desde Iquique, desde Arica. ¿Te has peleado con Joaquín? ¿La víspera de tu boda, Elvirita?... Hasta acaban de traer la torta.
>
> MAMAÉ ¿De tres pisos? ¿Como en la novelita de Gustavo Flaubert?...
>
> ABUELA ¿No vas a contarme qué pasa? Nunca hemos tenido secretos. ¿Por qué has quemado tu vestido de novia?
>
> MAMAÉ Porque ya no quiero casarme.
>
> ABUELA ¿Pero por qué? Hasta anoche estabas tan enamorada. ¿Qué te ha hecho Joaquín?
>
> MAMAÉ Nada. He descubierto que no me gusta el matrimonio. Prefiero vivir soltera.
>
> ABUELA ¿No te gusta el matrimonio? A mí no puedes engañarme, Elvirita. Es la ambición de todas las muchachas y también la tuya...
>
> ...

---

[13] *Linguistics for Students of Literature*, p. 250.
[14] *Linguistics for Students of Literature*, p. 247.

ABUELA (Avergonzándose) ¿Es por miedo, Elvirita? Quiero
decir, ¿por miedo a... a la noche de bodas? (La
Mamaé niega con la cabeza.) ¿Pero entonces por
qué? Tiene que haber sucedido algo terrible para
que plantes a tu novio la víspera del matrimonio...

MAMAÉ Ya te lo he dicho. He cambiado de idea. No voy a
casarme. Ni con Joaquín ni con nadie.

ABUELA ¿Has sentido el llamado de Dios? ¿Vas a entrar el
convento?

MAMAÉ No, no tengo vocación de monja. No voy a casarme
ni entrar al convento. Voy a seguir como hasta
ahora. Soltera y sin compromiso.

ABUELA Me estás ocultando algo grave, Elvira...

It is evident from this conversation, which we have taken the liberty
of reproducing in its entirety, that Elvira-Mamaé has violated what H.
P. Grice terms the Cooperative Principle in Conversation, namely the
conversational Maxim of Quantity: "Make your contribution as
informative as required."[15] As Mary Louise Pratt explains,"sometimes
communicative breakdowns are unintentional; other times people
genuinely choose not to fulfill the Cooperative Principle... People *lie*,
for example, or withhold information, or try to confuse the
addressee."[16] The Abuela's questions are not only requests or
commands to tell something: they are attempts to seek a meaning
behind the literal message. The Abuela plays at reading Elvira-
Mamaé's "unspoken" intentions by positing interpretations other
than, or in addition to, the literal meaning of what is said: "¿Es por
miedo, Elvirita? ¿Has sentido el llamado de Dios? ¿Vas a entrar al
convento?" Each question functions as a separate interpretation or
reading of the discourse. Her interpretations are also retellings of
what happened and thus, in a sense, other versions of Mamaé's story.
The effect upon the listener is a reaction to what the Abuela
considers to be a departure from the conventional arrangement of
storytelling: "Me estás ocultando algo grave, Elvira." Elvira, indeed,
does not inform because she cannot. Social pressures are acting upon
the speaker. Language is context-dependent, and Mamaé's use of
language can be fully understood only in terms of her speech
community, the repressive and traditional society of which she is a
part. The words of an utterance in life are to be taken as intelligible
not in themselves, or in relation to their speaker alone, but in relation
to a situation in response to which the speaker speaks.

---

15 Mary Louise Pratt, *Toward a Speech Act Theory of Literary Discourse*
(Bloomington: Indiana University Press, 1977), p. 130.
16 *Linguistics for Students of Literature*, p. 237.

As the characters engage in conversation with Mamaé or amongst themselves, the discursive level has a vicarious funtion with respect to the narrative level and aims at eliciting processes of expectation and forecasts from the listeners—a function also elaborated and displayed at the level of conversation between Mamaé and Belisario, as critical reader and interpreter of Mamaé's story concerning "la señorita." Below, for example, the characters are discussing the Abuelo's unfortunate encounter with street hoodlums when the topic of conversation is suddenly diverted.

ABUELO   Mi cabeza anda muy bien ahora. Les juro que sí, no he vuelto a tener el menor mareo. (Hace un gesto de pesar.) El sombrero y el... el aparato no me importan. El reloj, sí. Lo tenía más de quince años y no se había malogrado nunca. En fin, cambiemos de tema. ¿Oyeron el radioteatro de las ocho?

ABUELA   Lo oí yo, Amelia se lo perdió por estar planchando la ropa del futuro abogado. Figúrate que Sor Fátima colgó los hábitos para casarse con el compositor...

AMELIA   Ah, mira, tienes una herida en la muñeca.

ABUELA   Atacar a un viejo, qué cobarde.

ABUELO   Me cogió desprevenido, por la espalda. De frente, hubera sido distinto. Seré viejo, pero tengo dignidad y puedo defenderme. (Sonríe.) Siempre fui bueno peleando. En los jesuitas, en Arequipa, me decían "Chispillas," porque a la primera provocación, retaba a cualquiera. Nadie me pisaba el poncho.

MAMAÉ   (Volviéndose hacia ellos alarmada) ¿Qué dices, Pedro? ¿Retar a Federico Barreto por haberme escrito ese verso? No lo hagas, no seas fosforito... (44-45).

The empty spaces in the spoken text are invitations to the listener to fill in the gaps, to take "inferential walks,"[17] paralleling what the critical reader must do as he or she reads the written text.[18] The almost imperceptible transition in the Abuela's discourse from "real" to "fictional" marking ("Figúrate que Sor Fátima...") is a common

---

[17] Umberto Eco, *The Role of the Reader* (Bloomington: Indiana University Press, 1979), p. 212.

[18] As Wolfgang Iser notes: "... the blank in the fictional text induces and guides the reader's constitutive activity. As a suspension of connectibility between perspective segments, it marks the need for an equivalence, thus transforming the segments into reciprocal projections, which, in turn, organize the reader's wandering viewpoint as a referential field." *The Act of Reading* (Baltimore: Johns Hopkins University Press, 1978), p. 202.

occurrence in conversation as well as in written narrative, and again parallels the strategies used in the world of Belisario as composer, and ultimately at the level of the author's macro-text. The Abuelo's story, not unlike Belisario's self-reflexive commentaries on his own writing, displays a recognizable evaluative stance toward what is reported. The evaluation of a narrative is defined by some as that part of the narrative which reveals the attitudes of the narrator towards the narrative by emphasizing the relative importance of some narrative elements as compared to others.[19] The Abuelo's intent is not so much to inform as to narrate events and personal experiences which he believes are worthy of display and which serve a "self-aggrandizing" function.[20]

Another notable feature of the above conversation is its nonlinearity. It appears virtually impossible for any narrator to sustain absolute chronological order in an utterance for more than minimal length. The lack of chronological sequence in conversation parallels the nonlinearity of Mamaé's narrative, of Belisario's writing, and of the author's written text.

All forms of dialogue and communication run the continual risk of failure. The Abuelo's embedded narrative, wherein he relates an episode from his past, namely his youthful exploits as a dueler while a schoolboy in Arequipa, fails to secure the proper uptake in the listener. Mamaé, instead, imagines a situation which the signs "fui bueno peleando" and "retaba" have not explicitly denoted. The listener—because all spoken and written texts cannot presume to cater overtly to the possible range of its listeners and readers' dispositions—transforms a denotation into a connotation: "¿Qué dices, Pedro? ¿Retar a Federico Barreto por haberme escrito ese verso? No lo hagas, no seas fosforito. Fue una galantería sin mala intención" (45). Mamaé infers that Pedro will take on Federico Barreto, the poet, in a duel for having written her the love verses on her mother-of-pearl fan. Speech acts, then, like literary texts, give rise to indeterminacies. Reference to concrete situations in all discourse, spoken as well as written, must remain indeterminate—reconstructed by the listener or reader.[21]

---

19 William Labov and Joshua Waletzky, "Narrative Analysis: Oral Versions of Personal Experience," *Essays on the Verbal and Visual Arts.* Proceedings of the 1966 Annual Spring Meeting of the American Ethnological Society, June Helm, Editor (Seattle: University of Washington Press), p. 37.

20 "Narrative Analysis: oral Versions of Personal Experience," p. 34.

21 "As what is meant can never be totally translated into what is said, the utterance is bound to contain implications, which in turn necessitate interpretation. Indeed, there would never be any dyadic interaction if the speech act did not give rise to indeterminacies that needed to be resolved. According to the theory of speech acts, these indeterminate elements must

The poetic markings which underlie conversational discourse, such as "figúrate," point to the fictive dimension of all speech acts, including so-called normal speech acts.[22] The blurring of fiction and nonfiction through storytelling is summarized in the use of the verb *contar* interspersed throughout the text. In Spanish, the verb *contar* may be a synonym for *decir* (to tell, or to say, as to provide information), as well as *narrar* (to narrate, or to tell a story, "real" or "fictitious," in other words, to display a text). The indeterminate nature of *contar* is appropriate to the correlation between literary and nonliterary fictions. The overlap is evident throughout the text of *La señorita de Tacna*, where stories are hardly distinguishable from description or simple assertions. One example may serve to illustrate how, even at the level of conversation, *contar* has fiction-creating capacity. Belisario, in the following scene, discloses to Tío Agustín, the pragmatist in the family, his desire to become a poet.

> BELISARIO ... (Se dirige a Agustín.) Tengo que contarte algo, tío Agustín. Pero prométeme que me guardarás el secreto. Ni una palabra a nadie. Sobre todo a mi mamá, tío.
>
> ...
>
> No quiero ser abogado, tío. Odio los códigos, los reglamentos, las leyes, todo lo que hay que aprender en la Facultad. Los memorizo para los exámenes y al instante se hacen humo. Te juro. Tampoco podría ser diplomático, tío. Lo siento, ya sé que para mi mamá, para ti, para los abuelos será una desilusión. Pero qué voy a hacer, tío, no he nacido para eso. Sino para otra cosa. No se lo he dicho a nadie todavía.

be kept in check by means of conventions, procedures, and rules, but even these cannot disguise the fact that indeterminacy is a prerequisite for dyadic interaction, and hence a basic constituent of communication. Austin recognizes this fact at least indirectly by laying emphasis on sincerity as the main condition for a successful linguistic action: 'our word is our bond.' This condition makes two things clear: (1) The implications of an utterance are the productive prerequisite for its comprehension, and so comprehension itself is a productive process. (2) The very fact that a speech act automatically carries implications with it means that the fulfillment of the underlying intention of that speech act cannot be guaranteed by language alone, and sincerity of intention imposes clear moral obligations on the utterance." *The Act of Reading*, pp. 59-60.

[22] In support of this point, Mary Louise Pratt adduces the following examples: "The 'scenarios' in the Oval Office, the hypothetical situations used in mathematical problems and philosophical arguments, assumptions made 'for the sake of discussion,' speculation about 'what he'll do next' or

Agustín ¿Y para qué crees que has nacido, Belisario?

Belisario Para ser poeta, tío.

Agustín (Se ríe) No me río de ti, sobrino, no te enojes.
Sino de mí. Creí que me ibas a decir que eras
maricón. O que te querías meter de cura. Poeta es
menos grave, después de todo... (123-24).

Although this story remains at the level of ordinary discourse,
motivated by a desire to provide information, it too has a fiction-
creating capacity. Belisario's story incorporates an appeal to the
element of mystery and raises certain expectations in the listener.
Like the reader of a text, Agustín anticipates the conclusion, and his
final reaction matches that of a reader whose expectations have been
thwarted.

BELISARIO AND THE CONVERSATIONAL CONTAMINATION OF WRITING

The more "poetic" level of fictionalization in La señorita de Tacna
corresponds to the writing of the love story—that of "la señorita de
Tacna"—by Belisario. This level includes the first, modified, of course,
by the writer's own imagination. The self-conscious nature of writing
is simultaneously intensified and undermined through Belisario's
overt imitation of an oral performance. As Robert Kellogg explains it,
"When authors who can write imitate an oral performance, some
strange things result. The most obvious development in the case of
narrative art is the self-conscious narrator... When oral narrative
yields to written, the genuine oral performance becomes a
counterfeit: the acquisition of writing by authors encourages the
development of unreliable and ironic speaking narrators."[23] Like Don
Quijote emerging from the Cueva de Montesinos ("cerrados los ojos,
con muestras de estar dormido"), Belisario inhabits a special universe
where fiction is savored in all its guises.

In the same manner in which Mamaé and the other characters
engage in conversation in their private universe of discourse,
nonfictional yet simultaneously world-creating, so too Belisario will
set out to display his composition—the writing of the love story—by
engaging in conversation with Mamaé. Once again the act of
composition and the act of presentation are simultaneous. Because
written utterances are produced over a greater and flexible timespan,
subject to reflection, correction, and revision by the "speaker," once

---

'what might have happened if only...' are all fictional, as indeed are
imaginings, plannings, dreams, wishings, and fantasizings of almost any
kind." Toward a Speech Act Theory of Literary Discourse, p. 91.

23 R. Kellogg, "Oral Literature," New Literary History, 5 (1973-74), 59-60.

they are delivered to the addressee, they are fixed, and there is little possibility for clearing up misunderstandings or revising further. This type of written delivery has a great many consequences, one being that the writer regards the written text as more "authoritative" and definitive than spontaneous speech. Belisario's mode of composition, however, is essentially oral and automatic. Belisario composes what he says on the spot, speaking aloud to himself, making corrections as he goes, and revising or clearing up misunderstandings as the exchange with Mamaé proceeds. It is not a finished artifact, but a work in movement wherein speakers cannot be held accountable for what they say in writing.

In *La señorita de Tacna* there appears to be no distinction between "telling a story" and "having a conversation." Discursive strategies used by speakers in conversation are the same as those used by storytellers and writers of stories. Mamaé, in her retelling of "la señorita de Tacna" to little Belisario, who functions as the reader of her story, displays the same uncooperative stance evident in the previous conversations with the other characters. Mamaé's obstinate attitude is prompted by her relation to the listener. The child Belisario must only have access to material approved by uncontested preachers of social morality.

> MAMAÉ   ... a la señorita de Tacna el orgullo le permitía vivir, ¿ves? Soportar las decepciones, la soledad, la privación de tantas cosas. Sin orgullo, habría sufrido mucho. Además, era lo único que tenía.
>
> BELISARIO   No entiendo por qué le alabas tanto el orgullo. Si ella quería a su novio, y él le pidió perdón por haberla engañado con la mujer mala, ¿no era mejor que lo perdonara y se casara con él? ¿De qué le sirvió tanto orgullo: Se quedó solterona ¿no es cierto?
>
> MAMAÉ   Eres muy chico y no puedes entender. El orgullo es lo más importante que tiene una persona. La defiende contra todo. El hombre o la mujer que pierde eso, se convierte en un trapo que cualquiera pisotea.
>
> BELISARIO   Pero eso ya no es un cuento sino un sermón, Mamaé. En los cuentos deben pasar cosas. Siempre me dejas en ayunas sobre los detalles. Por ejemplo, ¿tenía malos tocamientos la señorita de Tacna? (101-02).

Mamaé's fictionalized history turned "story" conventionally marked and framed, like the previous conversational exchanges between herself and the other characters, provides for Belisario the listener an increased measure of cognitive interest at the expense of smooth and efficient access to information. Belisario, like the implied reader, displays an appreciation for what should be considered one of the essential characteristics of stories: "En los cuentos deben pasar cosas." This convention of storytelling establishes a framework of expectations that affect the speaker's sense of herself and the other listeners.[24] Mamaé, as "señorita decente" and as a reader of so-called decent literature, is constrained in her tale-telling, and Belisario's expectations are not met. The constraints of the speaker are evident in the modifications which the story undergoes, including the intentional withholding of information, and the merging of characters and situations. In the letter episode, for example, Señora Carlota— Elvira's old rival—and the Indian woman are fused into a single character, something which confuses and intrigues little Belisario, who is listening.

For the implied reader, the conventions of storytelling are modified by a further constraint: the notion of a story as an explicit topic which Belisario must come to terms with. The relating of a story or of a certain kind of tale becomes part of what Belisario and Mamaé talk about as they tell their stories, part of the theme of their utterance. The narrators then, in *La señorita de Tacna* make tale-telling an issue for themselves and their implied listeners and readers. Belisario and Mamaé's way of elaborating on this metanarrative provokes a running dialogue which serves as a discursive counterpoint to the events being recounted.

La señorita de Tacna's uniqueness and originality as a work of literature is also illustrated by the fact that it turns our attention overtly to that special relation of persons embodied in narrative speech. The relation is not just that of narrated characters to one another, nor simply that of "two parties" to narrative viewed as a "social transaction," the narrator and the listener. Though Barbara Herrnstein Smith conceives of narrative within a poetics of speech "as verbal acts consisting of *someone telling someone else that something happened*,"[25] M. M. Bakhtin makes us sensitive to the "third participant" her definition overlooks. Narrative may be better defined as *someone telling someone else that someone said or did or experienced something*.[26] The defining speech act of telling a story remains in effect in this definition. The listener's necessary presence is not lost, but the object

    24 Don H. Bialostosky, *Making Tales: The Poetics of Wordsworth's Narrative Experiments* (Chicago: The University of Chicago Press, 1984), p. 68.
    25 Barbara Herrnstein Smith, "Narrative Versions, Narrative Theories," *Critical Inquiry* 7 (1980), 232-33.

of the utterance is acknowledged as a third potentially speaking person—la señorita de Tacna—whose relation to the other persons, to the narrator Mamaé, who tells about her, and to the listener Belisario, who is interested in hearing about her, shapes the narrator's utterance.

> MAMAÉ   Y la pobre señorita pensaba, con los ojos llenos de lágrimas: "O sea que no me quiere a mí sino a mi apellido y a la posición de mi familia en Tacna. O sea que ese joven que yo quiero tanto es un sinvergüenza, un aprovechedor."
>
> BELISARIO   Pero eso no es cierto, Mamaé. ¡Quién se va a casar por un apellido, por una posición social! Que se quería casar con la señorita porque ella iba a heredar una hacienda, me lo creo, pero lo otro...
>
> MAMAÉ   Lo de la hacienda era falso. El oficial chileno sabía que esa hacienda la habían rematado para pagar las deudas del papá de la señorita.
>
> BELISARIO   Ya estás enredando el cuento, Mamaé...
>   Ya te fuiste otra vez por tu lado y me dejaste en la luna... (56-58).

In reading as well as writing we think the thoughts of another person. Whatever these thoughts may be, they must to a greater or lesser degree represent an unfamiliar experience, containing elements which at any one moment must be partially inaccessible to us, as "la señorita's" story is partially inaccessible to Belisario. As Belisario listens to Mamaé's story, he participates actively in the construction and reconstruction of, or "filling in" of gaps in, the text. The desire for harmonization and eventual removal of ambiguities from the text prompts Belisario (as it does the implied reader) to make certain deductions and inferences necessary to maintain the assumption, at

---

[26] "The topic of a speaking person has enormous importance in everyday life. In real life we hear speech about speakers and their discourse at every step. We can go so far as to say that in real life people talk most of all about what others talk about—they transmit, recall, weigh and pass judgment on other people's words, opinions, assertions, information; people are upset by others' words, or agree with them, contest them, refer to them and so forth. Were we to eavesdrop on snatches of raw dialogue in the street, in a crowd, in lines, in a foyer and so forth, we would hear how often the words 'he says,' 'people say,' 'he said...' are repeated, and in the conversational hurly-burly of people in a crowd, everything often fuses into one big 'he says... you say... I say...'." M. M. Bakhtin, *The Dialogic Imagination*, ed. by Michael Holquist, translated by Caryl Emerson and Michael Holquist (Austin: University of Texas Press, 1983), p. 338.

least, that, as in conversation, the speaker is observing the Cooperative Principle.[27] After listening to Mamaé recount that the Abuelo was guilty of some indiscretion which she at first seems unwilling to clarify to little Belisario, the latter surmises a story version of his own:

> BELISARIO (Escribiendo muy de prisa)   Te voy a decir una cosa, Mamaé. La señorita de Tacna estaba enamorada de ese señor. Está clarísimo, aunque ella no lo supiera y aunque no se dijera en tus cuentos. Pero en mi historia sí se va a decir (113).

Because every narrative version is constructed in accord with some set of purposes or interests, no narrative version can be independent of a particular teller and occasion of telling. Belisario's version of the story of "la señorita" is once again a function of, among other things, the particular motives that elicited it and the particular interests and functions it was designed to serve—namely the writing of a love story, with all the conventions which such a task imposes upon the writer.

READING AND WRITING AS CONVERSATION

What sort of communication do readers and writers complete in novels, poems, and stories? One could argue that the communicative act involved in literature is simply that of porjecting oneself into an imaginary world, the same projection as is involved in conversation. Belisario's job as reader (which precedes his task as writer) and the job of the real world reader outside the text is to contextualize the fictional discourse, that is, to infer information about the fictional speaker, speech situation, and world from the text. This is the process by which readers are said to enter into or "construct" the fictional world of a novel or other literary text. And to do this, readers rely on the same processes of deduction and inference they use in conversation. As we have· already seen in examples from the text, Belisario's writing is merely an extension of this process, an extension of Mamaé's storytelling, and of her ability to impersonate, anticipate and recreate audience reactions in advance. As Belisario soliloquizes: "No tengas meido, Belisario, aprende de la Mamaé" (58).

---

[27] The term *implicature* has been used to refer to various kinds of calculations by which a listener makes sense of what he or she hears. "What a speaker implicates on a given occasion is distinguishable from what he says, that is, from the literal and conventional meaning of the words he uses; what is said and what is implicated together form the meaning of the utterance in that context." *Toward a Speech Act Theory of Literary Discourse*, p. 154.

At the conclusion of his performance, his reading and his writing (his writing as reading), Belisario has not written a text; he has failed to write his love story: "No es una historia de amor, no es una historia romántica. ¿Qué es, entonces?" (146). If not a romance, then perhaps it is the story of a detection concerning another story, namely the story about the difficulty of writing a story, for Belisario's story has in a sense told itself.[28] It is a self-begetting story: "Nunca dejará de maravillarte ese extraño nacimiento que tienen las historias" (146). The love story as a completed text, a finished object, is displaced by the processes of reading it and of composing it aloud. Belisario is not a writer of stories, but a reader of stories, and as C. Lucía Garavito makes clear, La señorita de Tacna is not the writing of a story, but the writing of a reading.[29] Belisario, as reader-composer, finds greater interest in listening, in the imaginary dialogue which expresses Mamaé's dynamic relation with "la señorita," than in the writing, and in his conformity to readers poetic expectations.

Belisario recognizes that much of our enjoyment as readers is derived from surprises, from betrayals of our expectations. Mamaé's story aborts Belisario's hope for a love story and forces him to rely upon his own reality of experience and judgment, instead of upon extraneous literary expectations. The ending which includes the simultaneous death of the Abuelo (the aborted poet) and of Mamaé (the fabulator) constitutes an interesting conclusion. In reaching his own judgments concerning "la señorita de Tacna's" experience, Belisario as reader is restored to a kind of independence: independence of the "poetic," and independence of the text, since there is no written artifact, only the memory of a story, a work of the mind. For the implied reader, this independence translates into independence (a more difficult thing) of the Poet—of the writer, that is, as provider of new attitudes to life, of novel patterns and formulae of response.

By creatively experimenting with Belisario's guesswork as reader and his resistence to Mamaé's authoritative voice, Vargas Llosa suggests the importance of struggling with the influence that

---

[28] "La palabra tiene vida propia. Belisario trata de encauzarla pero termina dejando que la historia se cuente sola." Commentary by reader Myra Gann (State University of New York at Potsdam, and participant in NEH Summer Seminar, "Hispanic Drama: Social Contracts and Speech Acts," Summer 1984, State University of New York at Stony Brook, New York).

[29] "Curiosamente, un estudio de La señorita de Tacna pone de presente que el énfasis recae en el proceso de leer, al que se encuentra supeditado el de escribir. Se postula, entonces, dentro del proceso de creación, a la lectura como la actividad que subyace a la escritura misma, afirmación que está íntimamente relacionada con la retórica y con el concepto de manipular el lenguaje para lograr ciertos efectos," "La señorita de Tacna o la escritura de una lectura," 4.

"another's discourse," in M. M. Bakhtin's words, has upon an individual's coming to ideological consciousness.[30] The final rung, the intuition which stands (or more properly, on which the reader stands), because it is the last, is, of course, the rejection of written artifacts, a rejection that, far from contradicting what has preceded, is an exact description of what Belisario, in his repeated abandoning of successive stages in his argument, has been doing. But what, then, are we to make of the text of the play, itself—*La señorita de Tacna* as written by Vargas Llosa? Perhaps we can answer this question by considering once more its dramatic conventions.

CONCLUSION

It is ultimately the theatrical dimension of *La señorita de Tacna* which provides the key to understanding. The play is not just about reading and writing, and the writing of a reading. It is primarily about the *acting out* of readings, of writings, of stories. As Joaquín tells Mamaé after his aborted attempt to read the poems by Federico Barreto: "Aquí tienes el libro que me prestaste. Traté de leer los versos... pero me quedé dormido... Léelos tú por mí" (30-31), he articulates the displacement of reading and writing as private discourse in favor of reading and writing as public performance. Mamaé's response encapsulates what we can only suggest as theme: "Un día te los recitaré al oído y te gustarán" (31).

Reading, like theatrical representation, is essentially a performance which brings about a multiplication of communicational factors. Our minds as readers work the way Belisario shows his mind working, acting out a text, responding personally to persons. In reading, we imagine characters and narrators speaking; we experiment with tone of voice and gesture. We recognize words of an utterance not as the "thing" we are interested in but as a scenario of a certain event. The evidence of tone and gesture accompanying the scenario move us to

---

30 "This process—experimenting by turning persuasive discourse into speaking persons—becomes especially important in those cases where a struggle against such images has already begun, where someone is striving to liberate himself from the influence of such an image and its discourse by means of objectification, or is striving to expose the limitations of both image and discourse. The importance of struggling with another's discourse, its influence in the history of an individual's coming to idealogical consciousness, is enormous. One's own discourse and one's own voice, although born of another or dynamically stimulated by another, will sooner or later begin to liberate themselves from the authority of the other's discourse. This process is made more complex by the fact that a variety of alien voices enter into the struggle for influence within an individual's consciousness (just as they struggle with one another in surrounding social reality). All this creates fertile soil for experimentally objectifying another's discourse." *The Dialogic Imagination*, p. 348.

reproduce the event itself. The reader of literature, as Elias Rivers explains, "has to naturalize the text, has to do some of the archaic listenings."[31] Words are scripts into which the reader must read the tones that connect words with the situations they resolve.

Paralleling Belisario's simultaneous composition and presentation, in the theater composition and performance coincide—there is no text, only flesh and blood actors. The oral reality of the theater is several steps removed from textuality and "disembodied words."[32] By actualizing Belisario's performance as representation, Vargas Llosa postulates the theatrical possibilities inherent in all written discourse as well as the interrelationship between written and oral speech acts. Terry Eagleton, following Derrida, likes to point out that the "living voice" is, in fact, quite as material as print; and that since spoken signs, like written ones, work only by a process of difference and division, "speaking could be just as much said to be a form of writing as writing is said to be a second-hand form of speaking."[33]

If conversation can be viewed as another name for reading and writing *in* this play, then reading and writing as representation is the real title of this paper. Narration as representation also suggests itself as a possibility. The unique relationship between dramatic and literary discourse is recognized by Enrique Giordano when he states that "la virtualidad teatral es la virtualidad implícita a todo género literario y que se expresa en el mundo ficticio del lenguaje, mundo ya estructurado por la escritura."[34]

One final point suggested by the play, and illustrated perhaps in our use of the term "conversation," is that the features of individual narratives, including literary and fictional works, can be described and accounted for as functions of certain variables that control the features of all narratives, including nonliterary and nonfictional ones. *La señorita de Tacna* is one play, perhaps, in which literary narratives can indeed be real acts of narration, not just fictional speech acts.[35]

MICHIGAN TECHNOLOGICAL UNIVERSITY

---

[31] National Endowment for the Humanities, Summer Seminar: "Hispanic Drama: Social Contracts and Speech Acts," June 17-August 9, 1984, State University of New York at Stony Brook, New York. Note is from meeting and discussion of July 19, 1984.

[32] "Written dialogue reflects actual speech in a highly stylized form, of course; for example, physical gestures and vocal intonations, often essential in oral communication, can be represented in writing only schematically, if at all. But the ideal reader must be able to take into semantic account the context and situation of the imaginary speakers while comprehending as meaningful speech acts the text of their disembodied words." Elias Rivers, *Quixotic Scriptures: Essays on the Textuality of Hispanic Literature* (Bloomington: Indiana University Press, 1983), p. 138.

[33] Terry Eagleton, *Literary Theory, An Introduction* (Minneapolis: University of Minnesota Press, 1983), p. 130.

Works Cited

Bakhtin, M. M. *The Dialogic Imagination*. Austin: University of Texas Press, 1983.

Bialostosky, Don H. *Making Tales: The Poetics of Wordsworth's Narrative Experiments*. Chicago: The University of Chicago Press, 1984.

Culler, Jonathan. "Problems in the Theory of Fiction." *Diacritics* 14 (Spring, 1984): 2-11.

Eagleton, Terry. *Literary Theory, An Introduction*. Minneapolis: University of Minnesota Press, 1983.

Eco, Umberto. *The Role of the Reader*. Bloomington: Indiana University Press, 1979.

Elam, Keir. *The Semiotics of Theatre and Drama*. Methven: London and New York, 1980.

Garavito, C. Lucía. *"La señorita de Tacna* o la escritura de una lectura." *Latin American Theatre Review* 16 (1982): 3-14.

Giordano, Enrique. *La teatralización de la obra dramática, de Florencio Sánchez a Roberto Arlt*. México: La Red de Jonás Premia Editores, 1982.

Iser, Wolfgang. *The Act of Reading*. Baltimore: Johns Hopkins University Press, 1978.

Kellogg, R. "Oral Literature." *New Literary History* 5 (1973-74): 55-66.

Labov, William and Joshua Waletzky. "Narrative Analysis: Oral Versions of Personal Experience." *Essays on the Verbal and Visual Arts*. Proceedings of the 1966 Annual Spring Meeting of the American Ethnological Society. Seattle: University of Washington Press.

Martín, José Luis. *La narrativa de Vargas Llosa*. Madrid: Editorial Gredos, 1974.

Otero, Carlos-Peregrín. "Vargas Llosa: Teoría y Praxis." *Grial* 51 (1976): 18-34.

Oviedo, J. M. *Mario Vargas Llosa: la invención de una realidad*. Barcelona: Editorial Seix Barral, S. A., 1981.

Pratt, Mary Louise. *Toward a Speech Act Theory of Literary Discourse*. Bloomington: Indiana University Press, 1977.

Rivers, Elias. *Quixotic Scriptures: Essays on the Textuality of Hispanic Literature*. Bloomington: Indiana University Press, 1983.

Scholes, Robert. *Fabulation and Metafiction*. Chicago: University of Illinois Press, 1980.

Smith, Barbara Herrnstein. "Narrative Versions, Narrative Theories." *Critical Inquiry* 7 (1980): 213-36.

Traugott, Elizabeth Closs and Mary Louise Pratt. *Linguistics for Students of Literature*. New York: Harcourt Brace Jovanovich, Inc., 1980.

Vargas Llosa, Mario. *La novela*. Montevideo: Fundación de Cultura Universitaria, 1969.

—————. *La señorita de Tacna*. Barcelona: Editorial Seix Barral, S. A., 1981.

---

[34] Enrique Giordano, *La teatralización de la obra dramática, de Florencio Sánchez a Roberto Arlt* (México: La Red de Jonás Premia Editores, 1982), p. 22.

[35] "The theory of fiction needs to ... explore the possibility that literary narratives are, as in Pratt's first account, real world narrative display texts: not fictional speech acts but, if they must be acts at all, real acts of narration." Jonathan Culler, "Problems in the Theory of Fiction," *Diacritics* 14 (no. 1) Spring, 1984, 11.

Dramatic Speech Acts:
A Reconsideration

ALBERT PRINCE

VERYONE NEEDS HELP. Psychologists have looked to the characterizations of a Melville, Shakespeare, Proust or Cervantes for a better way to study the human personality. Similarly, specialists in literary criticism have turned to psychology and philosophy for ideas and concepts not available in their own field of study. The results have been spotty. For some, the application of a psycho-analytic, existential or Marxist view has proved useful; for others, these theories (or ideologies) are a needless and unsatisfactory digression from what they believe to be the best source of literary analysis, the text.

In the last fifteen years or so many literary scholars have begun to use ideas derived from the philosophy of language. Speech-act theory, the most influential philosophical contributor, has stimulated a variety of new assessments of dramatic literature. One of the main advantages of this theory is that it is a step toward the linguistic view of Wittgenstein (1953) and others in which there is a greater emphasis on the function of language as opposed to its structure. Further, this view emphasizes that what characters say in a drama is a worthy subject matter in its own right and that dialogue need not be constantly evaluated in light of the psychological and existential needs of the speaker or examined to see how well it conforms to the requirements of a Marxist state.

Unfortunately, there is often a mismatch between what speech-act theory has to offer and what literary critics want. In some cases, as Fish (1976) has shown in his masterly study of *Coriolanus*, the theory provides an unsurpassed framework for depicting the dramatic power of language. Conversely, with other dramatic works, the formalistic properties of speech acts are at odds with a subtle analysis of dialogue, plot and characterization.

Perhaps the origin of the theory in philosophy accounts for its limited application in literature. The logician prefers an idealized speaker whose every word follows a specifiable set of rules. It appears unreasonable, however, to make dramatic speech conform to the requirements of formal linguistics. I will try to prove this point by first discussing the controversy that led to speech-act theory, continue with a clarification of certain troublesome theoretical concepts, and conclude with an analysis of two Spanish Golden Age dramas (*Fuenteovejuna* and *La verdad sospechosa*).

In analytic philosophy, statements are classified as being either synthetic or analytic. Synthetic statements are subject to the verification principle and thus can, at least in theory, be evaluated as true or false. "Men are more intelligent than women" is a synthetic statement (it can be tested) and false (it has been tested). Analytic statements, on the other hand, are not subject to verification. The statement that volume equals length times width times height is true by convention or agreement. We say exactly the same thing when we refer to the cubic capacity of a room as volume or by its more wordy dictionary equivalent.

There are other assertions that are not so readily classified. An important example is the type of statement which appears to say something meaningful but does not fit either the analytic or synthetic category. A politician may claim that candidate X will be elected if he can convince the voters of X's sincerity. It may not be possible, however, to determine X's sincerity independently of the election returns. As a result the initial claim is reduced to the simplistic tautology—X will win if he gets enough votes. It is just this type of pseudo-proposition that analytic philosophy has done so much to expose.

While analytic philosophy has had the salutary effect of making us more and more aware of defective propositions, the price has been high. An increasing number of statements had to be labeled (technically speaking) nonsensical or meaningless despite their obvious importance in ordinary discourse or dramatic literature. There are many examples of assertions with great emotional force and profound impact that are empty of logical content when evaluated by strict analytic criteria, e.g., the ceremonial "I pronounce you man and wife" or the judicial "Case dismissed."

Philosophers have always known, of course, there were important imperatives and exclamations to be explained and that our language is permeated with promises, warnings, commitments and the like which can not be sensibly placed in the nonsensical category. The British philosopher J. L. Austin (1962) offered a novel way of looking at these dramatic assertions. He called them performatives, i.e., acts of speech the performance of which constitutes doing something. Performatives do not assert anything about a state of affairs but rather bring a state of affairs into being by declaring, promising, warning, etc. When a president declares a state of emergency, it is his words that bring that state into effect. The phrase "I sentence you to five years of hard labor" produces a tragedy; a child christened Egbert is put into a questionable status for life.

Performatives have a certain similarity to analytic statements; they are not assessed empirically but are evaluated by their degree of congruence with a pre-established and (ideally) institutionalized convention. Consider Creon's performative edict at the beginning of *Antigone*:

But his brother Polyneices ....
will have no ritual, no mourners,
will be left unburied, so men may see him
ripped for food by dogs and vultures
(Braun, 1973, p. 28: 237-242)

Creon's declaration is formally correct because certain constitutive conditions related to the power of government have been fulfilled: as the leader of the city-state of Thebes, Creon is empowered to issue such edicts; Polyneices is justly censured because he has betrayed the state; the edict has been promulgated according to law and carried out to the letter.

Austin used the term constative to refer to statements comparable to synthetic propositions. Constatives are usually a description of a state of affairs or a statement of fact, e.g., "It's raining" or "The window is open." When taken literally, these statements can be empirically evaluated as true or false. Complications arise when constatives are used metaphorically to make assertions that closely resemble performatives.

Recent research has made the distinction between analytic and synthetic propositions (Quine, 1961) difficult to sustain. Similarly, the performative-constative dichotomy did not survive Austin's rigorous examination of his own work. As a consequence he combined performatives and constatives into a single category called an illocutionary speech act. Two aspects of this category, the concept of illocutionary force and the distinction between direct and indirect speech acts, are especially important and will be considered in some detail.

Illocutionary force is not something a statement exerts (the metaphor is misleading) but something it has as part of a well established, usually social, convention. A speech act derives its meaning from being part of the convention and its force from the clarity of its concordance with the requisite components of the convention. Illocutionary force may be inferred, at least in part, by the degree of recognition or uptake on the part of the listener. A good example is the forceful reply of the chorusmaster to Creon's edict, quoted earlier:

Law and usage, as I see it,
are totally at your disposal
to apply to the dead and to us survivors.
        (Braun, 1973, p. 29: 250-252)

Creon's power is understood and, however reluctantly, accepted by all of the populace except Antigone. The dramatic power of the play comes from her struggle to retain her status as a member of the state and, at the same time, establish herself as an autonomous individual responsible only to a higher authority. Full membership in the Greek city-state demanded allegiance to a set of constitutive rules spelled out to the citizenry in their childhood. One can either accept legal convention or suffer exile and banishment.

It is in these dramatic, judicial-declarative, speech-act situations that Austin's concepts do so much to enhance our understanding of the power of performative language. This type of speech act exactly fits his remarkable thesis that language can bring into being the very conditions to which it refers. Language, to quote from Fish (1976), does not so much reflect the state in these instances, as that it is the state.

Indirect speech acts are those produced by linguistic constructions ordinarily employed for other purposes. In English the standard form of command is, of course, the imperative. Often, however, other constructions will do as well. In a cold room with a shivering speaker the icy statement "The window is open" will be recognized as a command to shut the window by most listeners. The fact that constative statements can so readily be used performatively is one of the major reasons the performative-constative distinction could not be maintained.

Another reason for the use of indirect speech acts is that the direct form entails a cumbersome sentence structure. Formal performatives usually have three basic characteristics: (a) they are almost always in the first person singular; (b) they frequently employ certain verbs, e.g., warn, promise and the like and (c) they often include the indirect object you. "I promise you I will do the best I can" is an example of the stilted language that results from strict adherence to the rules for performatives.

In most languages, assertions, commands, warnings, etc., can be expressed in a brief and casual way. In barroom, cafe and academic settings alike, listeners become impatient with excessively formal expressions and thereby discourage their use. Shown below are a few obvious but pertinent examples of how a formal assertion, warning and question can change to a comparable indirect illocutionary act.

DIRECT FULL PERFORMATIVE

I tell you it is raining.
I warn you, it is raining.
I ask you, is it raining?

INDIRECT TYPICAL SHORT PERFORMATIVE

It's raining.
It's raining!
It's raining?

Linguists usally account for the short, indirect, speech act by assuming the speaker recognizes the equivalence of the two forms and behaves accordingly. Another explanation, relying less on the rational powers of the speaker, is possible. Zipf (1935) showed that there is a marked tendency for almost all popular categories of speech to be shortened. Slang terms are usually shorter than the original, e.g., TV for television. Zipf explained this behavior by what he called the law of least effort, i.e., the less effortful a speech act the more likely it will occur. Thus, there is a strong tendency for accents to move away from the most frequently used speech sounds. Similarly, the clumsy and tedious direct speech acts are shortened because there is a payoff for the speaker. The short form of the performative, for most listeners, is equally clear and requires much less effort.

The shortened performative is not always advantageous for the speaker; it is sometimes curt and overly harsh in tone. This is especially true for imperatives. Fortunately, a command can be issued in a more gracious way in the form of questions, declaratives, warnings and other constructions. Some examples appear below:

DIRECT COMMAND Give me a hot dog!
QUESTION Would you be so kind as to give me a hot dog?
DECLARATIVE I haven't eaten a thing since breakfast.
WARNINGS If I don't get something to eat soon, I'll die of hunger.

Adult speakers usually (by no means always) recognize an indirect speech act and respond accordingly. Young children may not have acquired this level of sophistication as indicated by this well known example:

BOYFRIEND (*on telephone*) Hello, is Janice there?
YOUNGER
BROTHER Yes, she is. Goodbye. (*Click!*)

In experimental settings young children respond to such disparate requests as "Can you open the door?", "Must you open the door!" and "Should you open the door?" all in the same way—that is, by opening the door. It is only after a substantial exposure to a linguistic community in which indirect speech acts are valued that a child can be expected to understand the indirect message that is conveyed.

The dynamics of the indirect speech act reveal a major weakness in formalistic linguistic approaches to what people say. There is no place in such theories for everyday language that is not explicitly rule-governed. This is a significant omission because verbal practices are often shaped by the amount of effort required to say what we have to say, or by the demands of a given linguistic community. The patois, jargon, slang incorporated in much of our speech, both everyday and literary, result from social consequences far removed from the abstract rules and abstruse sentence structures that preoccupy so many linguists.

The explanations of indirect speech acts, proposed by linguists, assume that speakers are somehow inherently equipped for rational dialogue and that their speech is governed by a set of rules that permits them to deal with indirect speech acts as the occasion demands. The noted linguist, Noam Chomsky, is probably most responsible for the re-emergence of this ideal speaker concept. A similar conception was common in economics, political science and psychology some years ago. There was economic man who always spent his money wisely, political man who always voted rationally, and the average man who was said to represent everyone. These theoretical constructs never worked well in the social sciences, and it appears likely that conceptualizing a speaker free of human error and social influences will be equally unproductive.

Pratt (1981) has suggested that speech-act theory may be a way out of the realm of language as an autonomous, self-contained grammatical system isolated from a person's social environment. In a revised scheme, a speech act might be considered a type of verbal behavior largely determined by its social context and consequences. The case of a tourist visiting, say, a Spanish-speaking country is instructive. Many will use the speech-act "quiero" (I want) to ask for a service even though their guide books suggest the softer and more amiable "quisiera" (I would like). However, after a few encounters with the subdued but unmistakably resentful reaction of some of those who serve them, only the most ethnocentric tourist will refuse to switch to the more genteel form of request.

The gradual change in the type of verbal behavior exhibited by the new arrival has been studied extensively in psychology. It is simply the case that certain modes of expression are favored in a given verbal community. Sociolinguists could probably give a good account for many of these preferences and explain how they are encouraged. It is perhaps a bit easier to understand a particular verbal usage when it is disapproved. To go into a working-class tavern and say "It would please me ever so much if I could have a glass of sherry" is to invite contempt or something worse. The potential class conflict between such a request and the context in which it is made is readily apparent.

Despite the many difficulties, linguists appear reluctant to give up the notion of the ideal speaker. Grice (1969), for example, has proposed the Cooperative Principle, a set of assumptions that he contends all competent speakers bring to their conversational encounters. The basic ingredients of the Cooperative Principle are a set of maxims said to regulate the linguistic production of the speaker. If the maxims are followed, a speech act or a speech will be just the right length, relevant and succinct. The speaker will also be civil, truthful, and prepared to back up what he says.

Grice's ideas are central to a controversial issue in speech act theory—the distinction between constitutive and regulative rules. As indicated previously, constitutive rules are concerned with the necessary and sufficient conditions under which a speech act can be said to be felicitous. Coriolanus, contemptuous of the citizens of Rome to whose judgment he must submit, cannot meet the speech-act requirement to attain a consulship.

Regulative rules have been described by Hancher (1977) as specifying what is appropriate rather than what is necessary. To use Hancher's example—the bride's family customarily sits on the left while the groom's family sits on the right. This arrangement is regulative rather than constitutive because the marriage will be valid even if the families switch sides. On the other hand, the words "I pronounce you man and wife" are quite infelicitous if the groom has failed to dissolve a previous marriage.

Many of the recent applications of speech-act theory entail regulation rather than the constitutive rules that are at the core of the theory. Pratt (1981), for example, has suggested the theory be made more flexible by substituting the term "appropriate" for Austin's more stringent requirement of felicity. However, the term appropriate, as Hancher has so aptly observed, refers more to what is decorous than to what is logically essential. In upper-middle-class neighborhoods it is decorous to wear whites on the tennis court. A white outfit, however, can hardly be said to be a component of the game in the same sense as are the dimensions of the court or the height of the net.

It is, of course, possible to make a very useful analysis of the social contexts in which speech acts occur. It is also correct to say that speech-act theory was instrumental in leading literary analysis in this direction. But to describe this change in emphasis as a use of the theory is simply wrong. Austin's theory is based on formal logic, and thus its power is lost when there is not strict adherence to its basic tenets. Just as Marxist and psychoanalytic theories can be construed in ways to explain everthing, speech-act theory can be expanded to encompass all literary speech acts. Theories are often less useful when they "explain" too much than when they explain too little. "Small is beautiful" may be as relevant to literary theory as it is to the environment.

The penchant to invite speech-act theory in where it is not at home derives, in my opinion, from the disposition of students of language to view speech as governed almost exclusively by rules. Obviously some speech production is so governed. When I say to myself, prior to an introduction, "Professor Jones has a Ph.D. and must be addressed as doctor," I am following a rule of sorts. But most speech is not of this character. People chatter on for reasons unrelated to rules, even in literature. Young mothers (fathers), incarcerated with pre-lingual children all day, talk endlessly when their husbands (wives) arrive home. An attentive listener, especially someone attractive, will maintain and direct a greater quantity of speech than any set of linguistic rules. Theories, like Austin's, based on formalistic principles can not be readily modified to account for verbal behavior induced and maintained by its social context and social consequences.

A related difficulty with the theory is in the ambiguous definitions of the word "intention." In speech-act theory it is said to be a matter of what one takes responsibility for by performing certain conventional communicative acts. This suggests a public criterion for intention and implies that consideration of inner motives will be by-passed. At the same time we are told that what the speaker knows or believes about the situation confronting her and her purposes in saying what she says in the situation are essential for understanding a speech act. This apparent conflict is summarized by Searle (1979) in this statement: "Wherever there is a psychological state specified in the sincerity condition, the performance of the act counts as an expression of that psychological state. This law holds whether the act is sincere or insincere, that is, whether the speaker has the specified psychological state or not." This is the philosopher speaking: the psychological state may or may not be important and it may or may not exist.

Not everyone, I am sure, is ready to resolve this contradiction by adopting the radical behaviorist idea that intention is an explanatory fiction. Fortunately, there is an acceptable alternative based on some recent work in developmental psychology. In this research the term "intention" is not used to refer to a child's needs and desires. Instead, the term is defined by a complex sequence of actions, clearly observable, in which a speaker makes sure the listener is attentive, says something that requires a specific verbal response, and then carefully attends to the listener's response. If the response is not in accord with the stylized meaning that the child has acquired for this type of dyad, she modifies and edits her initial statement and resubmits it to the listener. The editorial change may or may not be said to reflect the original intent of the speaker, depending on the philosophical predilection of the person making the interpretation. In any event, original intent is not the key point; it is the public and meaningful verbal interaction between the two speakers that is crucial.

Public criteria of intention have a number of important advantages. First, inner motives are, to say the least, difficult to observe, and inferences about them are frequently a source of error. Second, public statements derive some of their power simply from the fact that they are voiced. A civil society expects and demands a certain correspondence between word and action; how else could a man's word be his bond? Insincere vows and false promises have a way of becoming sincere and true when exposed to public scrutiny. The person who makes a higher bid at an auction can not easily disclaim his action by pleading it was contrary to his private intentions.

A public criterion of intention also puts greater demands on the writer. She cannot overcome poor characterization by a simplistic attribution of internal motivation but rather must employ effective dramatic techniques. One device, frequently used by playwrights, is to manipulate uptake to indicate when a speaker's intentions are and are not fulfilled. *La verdad sospechosa* is a good example of a dramatic work in which uptake is a key element.

Don García, an affably romantic liar and nobleman, creates problems for himself, and interesting theatrical effects, by his imaginative tall stories. While almost everyone recognizes that he is lying, his charm, good looks, total lack of malice and ingenuous manner protect him from serious censure. His servant and tutor, Tristán, proclaims unctuous homilies against lying, but to little effect. This is because his moralizing is given in the form of a soliloquy at the end of a scene. The curtain falls before there can be uptake and the need to explain why a servant can so consistently lecture his superior is removed.

Uptake is handled skillfully with other characters as well. The father of Don García, Don Beltrán, is as pedestrian as he is pedantic. His statements receive either immediate and trivial uptake or no uptake at all. In the latter cases, he provides his own uptake by a tedious explication of his initial assertion. Dialogue involving Jacinta and Lucrecia, the two young and attractive female protagonists, entails a very different and convoluted form of uptake. Most of the

dramatic action in the play centers on the ambiguous consequences of
their speech acts.

The logical formalities of speech-act theory seem hopelessly out of
synchrony with the intricacies of this type of plot. Further,
examination of the text affords a better analysis of the play than
speech-act theory could provide. At one point Don Garcia gleefully
admits he is a liar. "Why shouldn't I lie?" he says, "What better way to
get everyone's attention?" Indeed, and what more plausible account
could be given of Don Garcia's verbal behavior?

Fuenteovejuna, in contrast to *La Verdad Sospechosa,* is a speech-act play.
The title is also the name of a hamlet caught in the political and
military machinations of an important period in Spanish history. The
most immediate threat to the community is a libidinous martinet who
demands, and often gets, sexual favors from the unprotected women
of the town. The notable exception to this regimen is Laurencia, who
will not acquiesce to the unwarranted demands of the comendador.
As the dramatic pace quickens, Laurencia gives a powerful speech
condemning the pusillanimous behavior of the townsmen. At the
height of her rage and contempt she makes metaphorical use of the
name Fuenteovejuna (sheep well) to strengthen her case. The enraged
townspeople attack and kill the comendador but then must face a
judicial inquiry ordered by the king. A townsman named Frondoso
asks Esteban, Laurencia's father and mayor of the town, what they
should say when they are questioned under torture. He replies:

ESTEBAN   If they ask who is guilty
             die saying "Fuenteovejuna" only.
             Not one word more.
FRONDOSO Nothing could be more straight.
             Fuenteovejuna did it. (Bentley, 1959)

"Die saying Fuenteovejuna" is a majestic speech act. The spokesman,
Esteban, weak and indecisive at the beginning of the play, has become
the courageous leader so badly needed by the people of Fuenteovejuna.

There is immediate uptake on Esteban's words, first by Frondoso,
and later by other townspeople including Mengo, the gracioso.
Fuenteovejuna is changed from a collection of passive, dispirited
individuals to a cohesive citizenry ready to die for a just cause. Even
the least among them (Mengo) is able to endure the rack while
responding to his inquisitors with the simple but eloquent
"Fuenteovejuna did it." The power of the word to establish a state
and a state of mind has rarely been so effectively realized in a
dramatic work.

To summarize this review, it can be said that speech-act theory
affords a good analysis of dramatic literature when certain

constitutive conditions are met, as in *Antigone, Coriolanus* and *Fuenteovejuna*. Those interested in certain other aspects of literary analysis may also find the theory helpful. In his study of *La Estrella de Sevilla*, Rivers (1980) points out the difference between an oral society's honor code and the more cynical code of a modern legal system devoted to written documents. In Lope's time the word of a nobleman took precedence over signed oaths and contracts. To ask for written confirmation of a promise wold be an infelicitous affront to the code of honor. The terminology of speech-act theory appears to be well-suited to this sort of historical comparison.

The major limitation on speech-act and other formal theories of language stems from the seemingly unanimous assumption that speech is exclusively governed by rules. True, the term rule in this context is a metaphor, but it is a metaphor that is seriously misleading. It is especially misleading in the implication that a speaker follows a set of instructions which she is not, in fact, following. If linguists and philosophers object to a literal conception of this term, it is up to them to account for the mysterious process of how a speaker follows an unstated, and often unstable, rule. Rules that must be heeded inarticulately, as Quine (1970) has so nicely put it, can hardly be said to enhance our understanding of language.

There are, of course, shared conventions of language that aid communication. These conventions, in all probability, operate less fully in everyday discourse than on the stage. If someone in a play says "I'm afraid I'm going to die," it is not too bad a guess to say he probably will die. The dramatist and her audience share a theatrical repertoire in this instance. The sharing of linguistic conventions is not as great, however, as many linguists would lead us to believe. The many citizens of Ohio who voted "no" only to find they endorsed an income tax would question the overlap between their conceptions of the English language and that of the lawyers who framed the tax proposal.

Speech-act and other theories of language have shown that what we say can be described by rules. This is not the same, as many appear to believe, as saying that speech is governed by covert instructions. We all stay pressed to the surface of the earth because of gravity, not in response to suggestions from Newton's equations concerning gravitational force. Distasteful as it may be to some students of language, there are similar forces at work on the way we speak.

MARIETTA COLLEGE

Works Cited

Austin, J. L. *How To Do Things With Words*, Oxford: Oxford University Press, 1962.

Bentley, E. *The Classic Theatre, Vol 3: Six Spanish Plays*, Garden City New York: Doubleday Anchor Books, 1959.

Braun, R. E. (trans.) *Sophocles*, London: Oxford University Press, 1973.

Fish, S. "How to Do Things with Austin and Searle: Theory and Literary Criticism," *MLN*, 91, 1976, 983-1025.

Grice, H. P. "Utterer's Meaning and Intentions," *Philosophical Review*, 78, 1969, 147-77.

Hancher, M. "Beyond a Speech-Act Theory of Literary Discourse,"*MLN*, 92, 1977, 1081-98.

Pratt, M. L. "The Ideology of Speech-Act Theory," *Centrum new Series*, 1:1 (Spring 1981), 5-18.

Quine, W. V. "Two Dogmas of Empiricism," in *From a Logical Point of View*, 2nd Ed., Cambridge, Mass.: Harvard University Press, 1961.

Rivers, E. "The Shame of Writing in *La Estrella de Sevilla*," *Folio* No. 12 (June 1980), 105-17.

Searle, J. "What is an Intentional State?" *Mind* 88, 74-92, 1079.

Wittgenstein, L. *Philosophical Investigations*, (trans.) G. E. M. Anscombe, Ox0ford: Blackwell, 1953.

Zipf, G. K. *The Psycho-biology of Language*, Boston: Houghton Mifflin, 1935.

DATE DUE			

Things done...   207186